Symfony 1.3
Web Application Development

Design, develop, and deploy feature-rich,
high-performance PHP web applications using
the Symfony framework

Tim Bowler

Wojciech Bancer

PUBLISHING

BIRMINGHAM - MUMBAI

Symfony 1.3 Web Application Development

First published: September 2009

Production Reference: 1150909

Published by Packt Publishing Ltd.
32 Lincoln Road
Olton
Birmingham, B27 6PA, UK.

ISBN 978-1-847194-56-5

www.packtpub.com

Cover Image by Vinayak Chittar (vinayak.chittar@gmail.com)

Credits

Authors

Tim Bowler

Wojciech Bancer

Reviewer

Jose Argudo Blanco

Acquisition Editor

David Barnes

Development Editor

Ved Prakash Jha

Technical Editors

Kartik Thakkar

Reshma Sundaresan

Copy Editor

Sneha Kulkarni

Indexer

Rekha Nair

Editorial Team Leader

Abhijeet Deobhakta

Project Coordinator

Srimoyee Ghoshal

Neelkanth Mehta

Proofreader

Lynda Sliwoski

Graphics

Nilesh Mohite

Production Coordinator

Shantanu Zagade

Cover Work

Shantanu Zagade

About the Authors

Tim Bowler has a Bachelor's Degree in Computer Science, a Masters Degree in Internet Technologies and e-commerce, and is currently studying for his Ph.D. in Near Field Communication. With over ten years of experience in web application development and agile project management, he has gained an MIET membership at the Institute of Engineering and Technology (IET) and Charted I.T. Professional membership at the British Computer Society (BCS).

Tim started his career developing web applications in PHP for a digital media agency in London. As client expectations and delivery times became more and more demanding, he introduced agile and scrum into the development process along with the Symfony framework, in order to effectuate rapid application development.

Tim is currently the Managing Director at Agile Labs (`http://www.agilelabs.co.uk`), which specialize in web application development and agile coaching.

I would like to thank all of my editors at Packt Publishing — Ved Prakash Jha, Srimoyee Ghoshal, Neelkanth Mehta and David Barnes — for this book.

I would also like to thank my parents, Marian and Michael Bowler, for inspiring me to do well and to achieve everything possible.

And finally, I would like to thank all of my friends for their patience and understanding that books don't write themselves.

Wojciech Bancer has a Master's Degree in Computer Science. He has over eight years of experience in web application development. In 2007, after passing the Zend exam, he gained a Zend Certified Engineer for PHP5 certificate. Wojciech started his career developing web applications in PHP4 and PHP5, as a freelancer. Later he started working for a digital media agency in London, where he was introduced to Symfony and the scrum process. Currently he is a Lead Developer at Agile Labs.

I thank all of the Symfony developers for their great work of creating the Symfony framework, making a PHP developer's life much easier.

I also thank Packt Publishing and my editors — Neelkanth Mehta, Ved Prakash Jha, Srimoyee Ghoshal, Reshma Sundaresan — for their kindness and support.

A special thanks to my wife, Kate, and my friends for their support and patience during long evenings spent on writing this book.

About the Reviewer

Jose Argudo is a web developer from Valencia, Spain. After finishing his studies he started working for a web design company. After six years of working for that company, and others, he decided to start working as a freelancer.

Now, after some years have passed, he thinks it's the best decision he has ever made, a decision that lets him work with the tools he likes, such as Joomla!, CodeIgniter, CakePHP, JQuery, and other known open source technologies.

For the last months he has also been reviewing Packt Publishing books, such as Magento Theme Design, Magento Beginners Guide, and others about to be published, such as Magento Development with PHP, Joomla! SEO, Joomla! and Flash, and a book on Symfony framework.

If that isn't enough, he is also writing a book on CodeIgniter for Packt Publishing, something that he is putting all his effort into.

To my brother, I wish him the best.

Table of Contents

Preface

Back in the days, PHP developers developed web sites using a mixture of PHP functional code and HTML, with no separation between the two. The problem with this is that larger sites lost scalability and maintainability. Not to mention that there was vast amount of code duplication. The increasing demand for web applications sparked a need for a better way of rapid application development.

A framework helps a developer to create code that is readable as well as maintainable. Further more, it helps to alleviate repetitive tasks by automating them and provides additional classes and tools to aid in rapid application development. The Symfony framework is one of the best frameworks available today. It contains all of the features mentioned in the previous sentences and even more. If Symfony doesn't have something you need, then by integrating external components you can achieve it quiet easily. By using the Symfony framework for your projects, you will be able to develop web applications quickly and more easily.

What this book covers

Chapter 1: Getting Started with Symfony gives an overview of the MVC framework and covers the key features of Symfony framework, such as plugins, generators, internationalization, forms, and validation that help to save time on development of an application.

Chapter 2: Developing our Application shows how to start developing an application with less effort by using the Command Line Interface (CLI). In this chapter, you will learn the basic activities, such as creating the folder structure and database schema, configuring the ORM layer, and generating models, forms, and filters. Finally, we will see how to build the database and handle the routing. We also learn to add styling to the pages and cover some common installation problems.

Chapter 3: Adding the Business Logic and Complex Application Logic shows how we can add business and application logic to make the prototype (created in Chapter 2) to interact with the database. In this chapter, become familiar with the flow of the MVC pattern in Symfony. You will see how a request is handled and passed to the the application logic, which in turn will retrieve data using models before passing the results to the view. This chapter also illustrates how to add plugins with an example of adding the DbFinderPlugin plugin to the application.

Chapter 4: User interaction and email automation introduces the Symfony subframework that handles forms. Here we will see how Symfony can generate nice looking forms for us, before creating our own formatting class. We then progress to create a fully customized form. We will also learn about how Symfony can be expanded to use the other third-party libraries, and how can we convert a module into a fully working plugin that can be packaged up and reused in other projects.

Chapter 5: Generating the Admin Area explains how we can build a backend admin area application without having to code much. In this chapter, we will initialize the Propel admin generator and customize it. Then we will see how to handle Foreign Keys using the admin generator. We will customize the layout and then secure the application by setting permissions for the user, and look at how we can handle credentials from the template.

Chapter 6: Advanced Forms and JavaScript contains examples on how to add JavaScript into Symfony, how to use more advanced widgets in forms, and how to handle M-N database relations. Finally we look at how to add AJAX support into your application.

Chapter 7: Internationalizing our Global Positions introduces internationalization and localization to parts of our application. In this chapter you will learn how to automatically set user language and how to allow the user to change their language. You will learn to create the XLIFF dictionary files using the Symfony tasks, which will help in internationalization and localization of the application. We will also see how to create the database to accommodate a multilingual site, and how Symfony handles the data retrieval for us.

In *Chapter 8: Extending Symfony*, you will learn to integrate components from other frameworks, such as eZ Components and the Zend Framework.

Chapter 9: Optimizing for Performance is all about optimizing our site by introducing compression and caching. We will start by looking at and using Symfony's caching framework. To take things a little further we then introduce a caching server. We will also look at several other useful tools that aid in speeding up web applications.

Chapter 10: Final Tweaks and Deployment introduces some of the ways to deploy web applications. Here we take a look at a better way to transfer applications than using FTP. We will also learn to customize the default error 404 and error 500 Symfony pages to match our site.

What you need for this book

LAMP or WAMP stack plus memcached installed. You will also need PEAR installed if you wish to installed Symfony via pear.

Basic knowledge of object-oriented design and ORM will be quite helpful.

Who this book is for

This book is for PHP web developers who want to get started with Symfony 1.3. If you are already using Symfony 1.0 or are new to Symfony, you will learn how to use it in the best way to produce better applications faster.

Conventions

In this book, you will find a number of styles of text that distinguish between different kinds of information. Here are some examples of these styles, and an explanation of their meaning.

Code words in text are shown as follows: "Open the `settings.yml` file, and then look for the `compressed` parameter key halfway down."

A block of code is set as follows:

```php
<?php use_helper('JavascriptBase'); ?>
<?php echo javascript_tag("
    function name()
    {
        //Code
    }
") ?>
```

When we wish to draw your attention to a particular part of a code block, the relevant lines or items are set in bold:

```
dev:
  .settings:
    error_reporting:        <?PHP echo (E_ALL | E_STRICT)."\n" ?>
    web_debug:              on
    cache:                  on
    no_script_name:         off
    etag:                   off
```

Any command-line input or output is written as follows:

```
$/home/timmy/workspace/milkshake>Symfony  generate:module frontend best
```

New terms and **important words** are shown in bold. Words that you see on the screen, in menus or dialog boxes for example, appear in the text like this: "As you can see in the following screenshot, the total page size is **113 KB**".

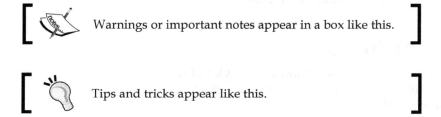

[Warnings or important notes appear in a box like this.]

[Tips and tricks appear like this.]

Reader feedback

Feedback from our readers is always welcome. Let us know what you think about this book—what you liked or may have disliked. Reader feedback is important for us to develop titles that you really get the most out of.

To send us general feedback, simply send an email to feedback@packtpub.com, and mention the book title via the subject of your message.

If there is a book that you need and would like to see us publish, please send us a note in the **SUGGEST A TITLE** form on www.packtpub.com or email suggest@packtpub.com.

If there is a topic that you have expertise in and you are interested in either writing or contributing to a book on, see our author guide on www.packtpub.com/authors.

Customer support

Now that you are the proud owner of a Packt book, we have a number of things to help you to get the most from your purchase.

Downloading the example code for the book

Visit `http://www.packtpub.com/files/code/4565_Code.zip` to directly download the example code.

The downloadable files contain instructions on how to use them.

Errata

Although we have taken every care to ensure the accuracy of our content, mistakes do happen. If you find a mistake in one of our books—maybe a mistake in the text or the code—we would be grateful if you would report this to us. By doing so, you can save other readers from frustration, and help us to improve subsequent versions of this book. If you find any errata, please report them by visiting `http://www.packtpub.com/support`, selecting your book, clicking on the **let us know** link, and entering the details of your errata. Once your errata are verified, your submission will be accepted and the errata added to any list of existing errata. Any existing errata can be viewed by selecting your title from `http://www.packtpub.com/support`.

Piracy

Piracy of copyright material on the Internet is an ongoing problem across all media. At Packt, we take the protection of our copyright and licenses very seriously. If you come across any illegal copies of our works, in any form, on the Internet, please provide us with the location address or web site name immediately so that we can pursue a remedy.

Please contact us at `copyright@packtpub.com` with a link to the suspected pirated material.

We appreciate your help in protecting our authors, and our ability to bring you valuable content.

Questions

You can contact us at `questions@packtpub.com` if you are having a problem with any aspect of the book, and we will do our best to address it.

Getting Started with Symfony

This chapter is an overview of the Symfony framework and how good it is to develop with. It will cover how Symphony conforms to the MVC pattern, the main features, general coding guidelines, and how to install it.

By the end of this chapter you will know:

- About the MVC pattern
- How Symfony incorporates the MVC pattern
- How to install Symfony

Exploring Symfony

Symfony was released in October 2005 by Fabien Potencier who is the CEO of Sensio, which is a French web agency (http://www.sensio.com). After Fabien used the framework on several projects successfully, he decided to release the project under an open source license. Ever since its first release, the Symfony community has increased dramatically and continues to do so.

The community can be found at http://www.symfony-project.org/.

The framework

A framework is aimed at reducing the development time without the need to sacrifice maintainability, scalability, or quality. Symfony can take less than a day to learn, comes with many tools and classes, and is easy to install. This means the developer can spend more time developing the application. All of these reasons and many more are why Symfony has come about, and why it has maintained its place as one of the best PHP5 frameworks.

The current trends at the moment seem to revolve around agile development methodologies with groups of developers working on the same web application. Using the Symfony framework, developers are aided in writing structured and maintainable code. This is all down to the framework's strict implementation of the **Model-View-Controller (MVC)** paradigm and modulization.

> *"It aims to speed up the creation and maintenance of web applications, and to replace the repetitive coding tasks by power, control and pleasure."*

More information about this project can be found at `http://www.symfony-project.org/about`.

The Model-View-Controller pattern

Many books go into the details of what the MVC pattern is and how it works. However, we will just look at the basic overview and how Symfony incorporates the pattern.

The MVC pattern is designed to split the presentation and business logic, and has a controller that manages the user's interactions between the two.

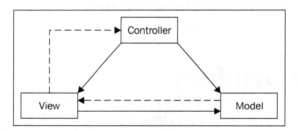

When you first use Symfony to generate the skeleton code for a new application and module, you can see exactly how Symfony strictly abides by the MVC pattern.

Controller

The **controller** is responsible for processing user events. The controllers in Symfony are split into several components.

1. It is the entry point into the application.
2. It determines what action is required to execute.
3. Loads the configurations.
4. Executes the filters.

One great feature about the controller being the entry point is that any time a site needs to go down for maintenance, the controller can simply be disabled. Creation of a new application in Symfony creates two controllers:

- A controller for the production environment
- A controller for the development environment

The difference between the two is the debug information and error displaying.

The controller calls an action, which is what drives the application. The action contains all of the application logic and has the ability to access everything from the request, sessions, authentication, and core Symfony objects.

Model

The **model layer** represents the applications data and the business rules used to manipulate and access it.

Symfony's model layer is split into two separate layers — an **Object Relational Mapping (ORM)** layer and a data abstraction layer. Of course, there are a few good PHP5 ORM and database abstraction libraries that already exist. Therefore, rather than reinventing the wheel, the framework incorporates the Doctrine ORM (`http://www.doctrine-project.org/`) which is the defualt ORM layer, with the option of using the Propel ORM (`http://propel.phpdb.org`). The second layer, being the data abstraction layer is handled by PHP Data Objects (PDO).

Database abstraction means database portability. Every database vendor will have a slight variant in their SQL syntax. Therefore, by moving your application to another RDBMS, a developer would have to amend certain queries. But with a database abstraction layer, this portability becomes transparent.

Object relational mapping turns database tables, rows, and different variable types into objects. As Symfony is written using OOP, it makes sense that the data is returned as an object.

At the moment, Symfony comes shipped with Propel 1.2 as it's default ORM. However, this whole ORM layer can be easily changed. For example, the ORM layer can be changed to Doctrine (`http://www.phpdoctrine.org/`).

Views

A **view**, which is commonly referred to as a template, is displayed to the user. These templates are completely separated from controllers and models. They mainly comprise of XHTML markup and presentation logic in the form of PHP tags. Although Symphony's template system has matured, the view layer can be replaced with another template engine, such as Smarty (`https://smarty.php.net`) through a plugin, for example.

Taking a look at the key features

We have looked at Symfony's implementation of the MVC pattern. Next, let's go over some of the features that Symfony has to offer in order to cut down development time.

Forms and validation

This is one of those repetitive requirements that a developer always has to face. Using Symfony, the development time is decreased due to the form subframework. There are two types of form:

- **Propel form** is a form that is based on a database table(s). These forms persist the submitted data to the table(s) that they are based on. As part of the generation task(s), these forms are automatically created along with validation. Although we can easily customize both form and validation, the default forms are a great way to display an initial prototype.

- **Simple form** is a form that doesn't persist data to the database. Although they are not generated, they follow the same approach as the Propel-based forms.

Plugins

One of Symfony's best features is its plugin architecture. So, many units of functionality can be written as a plugin and used time and again. The available plugins either help a developer in some way, or provide full, feature-rich applications. Looking at the plugin repository, numerous plugins have been submitted by the community and it continues to grow. You can visit `http://trac.symfony-project.com/wiki/SymfonyPlugins` to know more about Symfony Plugins. A few of the main plugins are:

- `sfGuardPlugin`: Web asset management
- `sfSimpleBlog`: Simple blog for your site
- `sfSimpleCMSPlugin`: Create a CMS
- `sfLucenePlugin`: Integrates the Zend framework's search engine

Internationalization and localization

Many web applications offer locale translations and services based on your locale. Symfony provides interfaces, standards, and localized helpers to make internationalization (i18N) and localization (l10N) simple.

There are two places where time is cut down. The first is by using XLIFF dictionary files for static template text. Wrapping sentences or words inside a special helper function will automatically do all the lookups in the dictionary files. Also, using a task on the command line, will do all of this for you. The second place is within the ORM layer, which provides additional methods for I18N lookups.

Generators

When writing a web application, more often than not, a backend administration area is needed to manage content. This can increase development time dramatically. Symfony has generators which when run from a task on the command line can scaffold forms on the front end and also backend administration forms. These forms are based on a model, just like when creating normal forms. Not only are the forms created, but also all of the code to provide a form with the ability to **Create Retrieve Update** and **Delete** (**CRUD**) records in the database. The backend-generated forms also use a theme to create better-looking forms.

Cache

Cache is the fastest method of retrieving information. In Symfony, templates, partials, components, and actions can all be cached to speed up the response times. Configuration of the cache is also governed by a configuration file. Although there are a few configuration YAML files, they are all converted into PHP arrays and cached the first time the application runs. By default the cache is stored on the file system, but a small amend to one of the configuration files can easily swap this to another caching mechanism such as memcache, for example.

Testing

Test-driven development is the key to bug-free and well-written code. Symfony provides the ability for unit and functional testing. Unit tests enable the developer to test functions and methods for input and output. While functionality tests helps the developer to test for functional issues that would be executed in the browser, Symfony has its own testing framework called **Lime**. This testing framework is useful for both unit testing and functional testing. All test output can be saved in the xUnit format.

Configuration files

By default, all the files are written in the YAML format (`http://www.yaml.org/`). When first run, the configuration is read and then written to cache as a native PHP array. Many of Symfony's features are customizable in the many configuration files.

As you can see, Symfony is a solid framework that contains many features, is dynamic, and more importantly, cuts down development time. Also, parts of Symfony can be extended, replaced with a plugin and provides a bridge for other frameworks, which we will look at later.

Coding guidelines

One thing that I have learned in the past is to always establish coding guidelines. Following some of the eXtreme programming principles—namely, pair programming—I have learned that having a set of guidelines helps team integration and code readability.

Symfony-specific guidelines

These are some Symfony-specific guidelines:

- One module is not for one page. The only time where this might be ruled out is if there is a strong possibility of the module being extended.

  For instance, if you have general footer pages, these could be a part of the general module. Also, grouping functionality allows code to be refactored into a plugin during development.

- Application-specific settings should always go in the app.yml file.

- When using a mail plugin for sending out emails, abide by the MVC pattern.

  That means use the action and templates rather than storing content inside a variable.

- Keep PHP to an absolute minimum within templates.

- Database table names should be plural and PHP models names should be singular.

Installing Symfony

There are three ways in which you can install and set up Symfony on your local system:

- Using the sandbox
- Checking out of subversion
- Installing via PEAR

Version 1.3 was not released at the time of the writing this book, so I cannot provide you with the exact links to install it. However, I can point you in the direction of some more useful documentation located on the Symfony web site at `http://www.symfony-project.org/installation` and `http://www.symfony-project.org/getting-started/1_2/en/`.

The fastest way of setting up Symfony, especially for the first time, is to download the sandbox. The sandbox works straight out of box and contains the basic application already created for you.

The sandbox can be downloaded from `http://www.symfony-project.org/get/symfony-stable.tgz` 0.

If you follow the PEAR route, you can use that installation to create your own sandbox at `http://www.symfony-project.org/blog/2009/06/10/new-in-symfony-1-3-project-creation-customization`.

For developing with Version 1.3, I used two methods to obtain a sandbox. Checked out Symfony from SVN into a temporary folder:

```
>mkdir symfony_1.3 && cd symfony_1.3
>svn co http://svn.symfony-project.com/branches/1.3
```

Next I used the Symfony `create_sandbox` script to create a zipped up sandbox:

```
>data/bin/create_sandbox.sh
```

After running the command you will see the package being build. Afterwards, you will see two new files in the current folder, `sf_sandbox.tgz` and `sf_sandbox.zip`. You can extract either one and rename the folder from `sf_sandbox` to `milkshake`. Afterwards you can place this folder in your `workspace` folder.

Summary

In this chapter, we saw the MVC framework and an overview of some of Symfony's key features that help to save time on development. These features consisted of plugins, generators, internationalization, forms and validation.

We can see how simple it is to get Symfony up and running on our local computer. Being eager to start, get ready for the coming chapters.

2
Developing Our Application

Developing an application in Symfony is easy and time-saving, and one of the best ways to demonstrate that is to create a web site. In this chapter, we begin our journey by jumping straight into development. By the end of this chapter, we will have an initial prototype, which will serve as a starting point for the other chapters.

Along the way you will be introduced to the MVC flow within Symfony where you will understand about the business and application logic, and designing the database.

In this chapter you will learn how to:

- Set up the foundations for a basic database-driven web site using the Symfony framework
- Use some of the available Symfony tasks to cut out repetition
- Create a database schema and later understand its relation to the ORM and forms
- Understand the flow of the request to the controller, action, routing, and template rendering

The milkshake shop

Our application will be designed for a fictitious milkshake shop. The functional requirements for our shop are:

- Display of the menu, job vacancies, and locations; these details will be updated from the back office
- Sign up to a newsletter, where users can submit their details
- Search facility for the menu
- Secure backend for staff to update the site
- The site must be responsive
- Option for the users to view our vacancies in three languages

Creating the skeleton folder structure

Symfony has many ways in which it can help the developer create applications with less efforts — one way is by using the Symfony tasks available on the **Command Line Interface** (**CLI**). We will be using this method extensively in this book. These Symfony tasks do the following:

- Generate the folder structure for your project, modules, applications, and tasks
- Clear the generated cache and rotate log files
- Create controllers to enable and disable an application and set permissions
- Interact with the ORM layer to build models and forms
- Interact with SQL to insert data into the database
- Generate initial tests and execute them
- Search for text in your templates that need i18N dictionaries and create them

 If you'd like to see all the tasks that are available with Symfony, just type the following on your command line:
`symfony`

Let's begin with using one of the *Symfony tasks to generate the file structure* for our project. Our project will reside in the `milkshake` folder. In your terminal window, change your folder path to the path that will hold your project and create this `milkshake` folder. My folder will reside in `workspace` folder. Therefore, I would type this:

```
$mkdir ~/workspace/milkshake && cd ~/workspace/milkshake
```

Now that I have the project folder and have changed the path to within the `milkshake` folder, let's use a Symfony task to generate the project file structure. In your terminal window, type the following:

```
$/home/timmy/workspace/milkshake>symfony generate:project -orm=Propel
milkshake
```

We can generate our project we can also specify which ORM we would like to use. Our application is going to use the Propel ORM, but you can also opt for Doctrine ORM. By default, Doctrine ORM is enabled.

After pressing the *Enter* key, the task goes into action. Now you will see output like the one in the following screenshot on your terminal window. This screenshot shows the folder structure being created:

```
timmy@timmys-laptop:~/workspace/milkshake$ symfony generate:project --orm=Propel milkshake
>> dir+       /home/timmy/workspace/milkshake/doc
>> dir+       /home/timmy/workspace/milkshake/plugins
>> dir+       /home/timmy/workspace/milkshake/lib
>> dir+       /home/timmy/workspace/milkshake/lib/form
>> file+      /home/timmy/workspace/milkshake/lib/form/BaseForm.class.php
>> file+      /home/timmy/workspace/milkshake/symfony
>> dir+       /home/timmy/workspace/milkshake/web
>> file+      /home/timmy/workspace/milkshake/web/.htaccess
>> file+      /home/timmy/workspace/milkshake/web/robots.txt
>> dir+       /home/timmy/workspace/milkshake/web/js
>> dir+       /home/timmy/workspace/milkshake/web/uploads
>> dir+       /home/timmy/workspace/milkshake/web/uploads/assets
>> dir+       /home/timmy/workspace/milkshake/web/images
>> dir+       /home/timmy/workspace/milkshake/web/css
>> file+      /home/timmy/workspace/milkshake/web/css/main.css
>> dir+       /home/timmy/workspace/milkshake/cache
>> dir+       /home/timmy/workspace/milkshake/apps
>> dir+       /home/timmy/workspace/milkshake/data
>> dir+       /home/timmy/workspace/milkshake/data/fixtures
>> file+      /home/timmy/workspace/milkshake/data/fixtures/fixtures.yml
>> dir+       /home/timmy/workspace/milkshake/test
>> dir+       /home/timmy/workspace/milkshake/test/unit
>> dir+       /home/timmy/workspace/milkshake/test/bootstrap
>> file+      /home/timmy/workspace/milkshake/test/bootstrap/functional.php
>> file+      /home/timmy/workspace/milkshake/test/bootstrap/unit.php
>> dir+       /home/timmy/workspace/milkshake/test/functional
>> dir+       /home/timmy/workspace/milkshake/config
>> file+      /home/timmy/workspace/milkshake/config/rsync_exclude.txt
>> file+      /home/timmy/workspace/milkshake/config/properties.ini
>> file+      /home/timmy/workspace/milkshake/...g/ProjectConfiguration.class.php
>> dir+       /home/timmy/workspace/milkshake/log
>> tokens     /home/timmy/workspace/milkshake/config/rsync_exclude.txt
>> tokens     /home/timmy/workspace/milkshake/config/properties.ini
>> tokens     /home/timmy/workspace/milkshake/...g/ProjectConfiguration.class.php
>> tokens     /home/timmy/workspace/milkshake/config/rsync_exclude.txt
>> tokens     /home/timmy/workspace/milkshake/config/properties.ini
>> tokens     /home/timmy/workspace/milkshake/...g/ProjectConfiguration.class.php
>> tokens     /home/timmy/workspace/milkshake/lib/form/BaseForm.class.php
>> file+      /home/timmy/workspace/milkshake/config/schema.yml
>> file+      /home/timmy/workspace/milkshake/config/propel.ini
>> file+      /home/timmy/workspace/milkshake/config/databases.yml
>> sfPearFrontendPlugin Attempting to discover channel "pear.symfony-project.com"...
>> sfPearFrontendPlugin downloading channel.xml ...
>> sfPearFrontendPlugin Starting to download channel.xml (663 bytes)
>> sfPearFrontendPlugin
>> sfPearFrontendPlugin ...done: 663 bytes
>> sfPearFrontendPlugin Auto-discovered channel "pear.symfony-project.com", alias
>> sfPearFrontendPlugin "symfony", adding to registry
>> sfPearFrontendPlugin Attempting to discover channel
>> sfPearFrontendPlugin "plugins.symfony-project.org"...
>> sfPearFrontendPlugin downloading channel.xml ...
>> sfPearFrontendPlugin Starting to download channel.xml (639 bytes)
>> sfPearFrontendPlugin ...done: 639 bytes
>> sfPearFrontendPlugin Auto-discovered channel "plugins.symfony-project.org", alias
>> sfPearFrontendPlugin "symfony-plugins", adding to registry
>> chmod 777 /home/timmy/workspace/milkshake/web/uploads
>> chmod 777 /home/timmy/workspace/milkshake/cache
>> chmod 777 /home/timmy/workspace/milkshake/log
>> chmod 777 /home/timmy/workspace/milkshake/symfony
>> chmod 777 /home/timmy/workspace/milkshake/cache/.pear
>> chmod 777 /home/timmy/workspace/milkshake/web/uploads/assets
>> tokens     /home/timmy/workspace/milkshake/config/schema.yml
>> tokens     /home/timmy/workspace/milkshake/config/rsync_exclude.txt
>> tokens     /home/timmy/workspace/milkshake/config/properties.ini
>> tokens     /home/timmy/workspace/milkshake/config/propel.ini
>> tokens     /home/timmy/workspace/milkshake/config/databases.yml
>> tokens     /home/timmy/workspace/milkshake/...g/ProjectConfiguration.class.php
>> tokens     /home/timmy/workspace/milkshake/lib/form/BaseForm.class.php
```

Let's have a look at the top-level folders that have been created in our project folder:

Folders	Description
apps	This folder contains our frontend application and any other applications that we will create
batch	If there are any batch scripts, they are placed here
cache	This folder is the location for cached files and/or scaffolded modules
config	This folder holds all the main configuration files and the database schema definitions
data	This folder holds data files such as test or fixture data
doc	All our documentation should be stored in this folder; this includes briefs, PhpDoc for API, Entity Relationship Diagrams, and so on
lib	Our models and classes are located in this folder so that all applications can access them
log	This folder holds the development controllers log files and our Apache log
plugins	All installed plugins are located in this folder
test	All unit and functional tests should be placed in this folder; Symfony will create and place stubs in this folder when we create our modules
web	This is the web root folder that contains all web resources such as images, CSS, JavaScript, and so on

There are three folders that must be writable by the web server. These are the cache, log, and web/uploads/. If these are not writable to your web server, then the server itself will either produce warnings at startup or fail to start. The files permissions are usually set during the generation process, but sometimes this can fail. You can use the following task to set the permissions:

```
$/home/timmy/workspace/milkshake>symfony project:
permissions
```

With the initial project skeleton built, next we must create an **application**. Symfony defines an application as operations that are grouped logically and that can run independent of one another. For example, many sites have a frontend and back office/admin area. The admin area is where a user logs in and updates areas on the frontend. Of course, our application will also provide this functionality. We will call these areas frontend and backend. Our first application is going to be the frontend. Again, let's use a Symfony task to generate the frontend application folder structure. Enter the following task in your terminal window:

```
$/home/timmy/workspace/milkshake>symfony generate:app frontend
```

Again, after executing this task, you will see the following in your terminal window:

```
timmy@timmys-laptop:~/workspace/milkshake$ symfony generate:app frontend
>> dir+        /home/timmy/workspace/milkshake/apps/frontend/lib
>> file+       /home/timmy/workspace/milkshake...s/frontend/lib/myUser.class.php
>> dir+        /home/timmy/workspace/milkshake/apps/frontend/i18n
>> dir+        /home/timmy/workspace/milkshake/apps/frontend/modules
>> dir+        /home/timmy/workspace/milkshake/apps/frontend/templates
>> file+       /home/timmy/workspace/milkshake...s/frontend/templates/layout.php
>> dir+        /home/timmy/workspace/milkshake/apps/frontend/config
>> file+       /home/timmy/workspace/milkshake/apps/frontend/config/filters.yml
>> file+       /home/timmy/workspace/milkshake/apps/frontend/config/routing.yml
>> file+       /home/timmy/workspace/milkshake...ps/frontend/config/security.yml
>> file+       /home/timmy/workspace/milkshake/apps/frontend/config/app.yml
>> file+       /home/timmy/workspace/milkshake...s/frontend/config/factories.yml
>> file+       /home/timmy/workspace/milkshake...ps/frontend/config/settings.yml
>> file+       /home/timmy/workspace/milkshake/apps/frontend/config/view.yml
>> file+       /home/timmy/workspace/milkshake/apps/frontend/config/cache.yml
>> file+       /home/timmy/workspace/milkshake...licationConfiguration.class.php
>> tokens      /home/timmy/workspace/milkshake...ps/frontend/config/settings.yml
>> file+       /home/timmy/workspace/milkshake/web/index.php
>> file+       /home/timmy/workspace/milkshake/web/frontend_dev.php
>> tokens      /home/timmy/workspace/milkshake/web/index.php
>> tokens      /home/timmy/workspace/milkshake/web/frontend_dev.php
>> rename      /home/timmy/workspace/milkshake...frontendConfiguration.class.php
>> tokens      /home/timmy/workspace/milkshake...frontendConfiguration.class.php
>> chmod 777   /home/timmy/workspace/milkshake/web/uploads
>> chmod 777   /home/timmy/workspace/milkshake/cache
>> chmod 777   /home/timmy/workspace/milkshake/log
>> chmod 777   /home/timmy/workspace/milkshake/symfony
>> chmod 666   /home/timmy/workspace/milkshake/cache/project_autoload.cache
>> chmod 777   /home/timmy/workspace/milkshake/web/uploads/assets
>> dir+        /home/timmy/workspace/milkshake/test/functional/frontend
```

Let's have a look at the top-level folders that have just been created in the `apps` folder:

Directory	Description
config	This folder will have all configuration files for our application
i18N	This folder will contain all Internationalization files
lib	This folder will hold all application-specific classes
modules	All our modules will be built in this folder
templates	The default layout template is created in this folder, and any other global templates that will be created will also be placed in this folder

These steps will generate our project and frontend application folder structure, and we can now view our project in a web browser. Open your web browser and go to `http://milkshake/frontend_dev.php` and you will see the following default Symfony page:

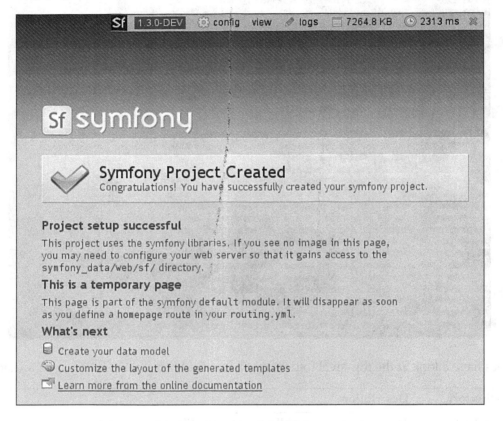

Now we can see the default project page along with the instructions on what to do next. The `frontend_dev.php` file is our index file while developing the frontend application, and adheres to the naming convention of `<application>_<environment>.php`. This **controller** is the development controller and is rather helpful while developing. Before we continue though, I urge you to also have a look at the web debug toolbar. We will be covering this later in this book.

Creating our database schema

When you think of creating the database schema, what generally springs to mind is either SQL CREATE statements or using a client such as phpMyAdmin to create the schema. But in Symfony, we will create the schema in either YAML or XML. For our application, we will be using the XML for a few reasons:

- XML schemas are arguably easier to read than YAML schemas
- Susceptibility of YAML to whitespace errors is exaggerated in these larger configuration files, and sometimes there is fall over with very large databases

Our schema may appear as though it's only for the database, but it is also a part of the ORM and forms generation process. As you can imagine, the schema is important for the integrity of our application.

Our database will be fairly simple. We will need to hold data for the milkshakes, flavors, store locations, vacancies, and user sign-up details. For visual reference, the entity relationship diagram is shown as follows:

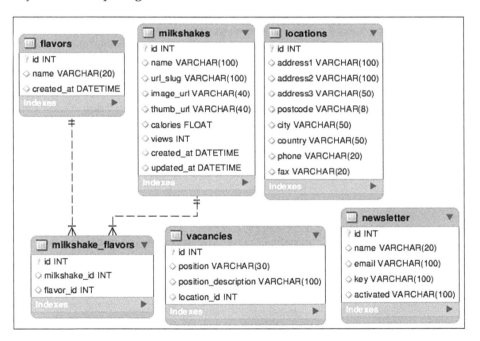

By default, Symfony only generates a schema.yml file that is located in the config folder. As we want to create our schema using XML, simply rename the existing schema.yml file to schema.xml. Once you have done that, copy in the following schema:

```xml
<?xml version="1.0" encoding="UTF-8"?>
<database name="propel" defaultIdMethod="native"
        noXsd="true" package="lib.model">

    <table name="milkshakes" idMethod="native"
        phpName="Milkshake">

        <column name="id" type="INTEGER"
                required="true" autoIncrement="true"
                primaryKey="true" index="true" />
        <column name="name" type="VARCHAR"
                size="100" required="true" index="true"  />
        <column name="URL_slug" type="VARCHAR"
                size="100" required="true" />
        <column name="image_URL" type="VARCHAR"
                size="40" required="true" />
        <column name="thumb_URL" type="VARCHAR"
                size="40" required="true" />
        <column name="calories" type="FLOAT" required="true" />
        <column name="views" type="INTEGER" default="0"/>
        <column name="created_at" type="TIMESTAMP" required="true" />
        <column name="updated_at" type="TIMESTAMP" required="true" />

        <index name="milkshake_name_index">
            <index-column name="name"/>
        </index>
    </table>

    <table name="flavors" idMethod="native" phpName="Flavor">

        <column name="id" type="INTEGER" required="true"
                autoIncrement="true" primaryKey="true" />
        <column name="name" type="VARCHAR"
                size="20" required="true" />
        <column name="created_at" type="TIMESTAMP" required="true" />
    </table>

    <table name="milkshake_flavors" idMethod="native"
        phpName="MilkshakeFlavor">
        <column name="id" type="INTEGER" required="true"
                autoIncrement="true" primaryKey="true" />
        <column name="milkshake_id" type="INTEGER" required="true" />
        <column name="flavor_id" type="INTEGER" required="true" />
```

```
            <foreign-key foreignTable="flavors" onDelete="CASCADE">
                <reference local="flavor_id" foreign="id" />
            </foreign-key>

            <foreign-key foreignTable="milkshakes" onDelete="CASCADE">
                <reference local="milkshake_id" foreign="id" />
            </foreign-key>
        </table>

        <table name="store_locations" idMethod="native"
                phpName="StoreLocation">

            <column name="id" type="INTEGER" required="true"
                    autoIncrement="true" primaryKey="true" />
            <column name="address1" type="VARCHAR"
                    size="100" required="true" />
            <column name="address2" type="VARCHAR"
                    size="100" required="true" />
            <column name="address3" type="VARCHAR"
                    size="50" required="true" />
            <column name="postcode" type="VARCHAR"
                    size="8" required="true" />
            <column name="city" type="VARCHAR"
                    size="50" required="true" />
            <column name="country" type="VARCHAR"
                    size="50" required="true" />
            <column name="phone" type="VARCHAR"
                    size="20" required="true" />
            <column name="fax" type="VARCHAR"
                    size="20" required="true" />
        </table>

        <table name="vacancies" idMethod="native" phpName="Vacancy">

            <column name="id" type="INTEGER" required="true"
                    autoIncrement="true" primaryKey="true" />
            <column name="position" type="VARCHAR"
                    size="30" required="true" />
            <column name="position_description" type="VARCHAR"
                    size="100" required="true" />
            <column name="location_id" type="INTEGER" required="true" />

            <foreign-key foreignTable="store_locations"
                        onDelete="CASCADE">

                <reference local="location_id" foreign="id" />
            </foreign-key>
        </table>
    </database>
```

When creating our schema, it is important to stick to the Propel and Symfony naming conventions — all table names should be plural and all models should be singular. The reason for this is that all the methods names are generated and have s appended to the function name. To retrieve all milkshake flavors, we would call the `getMilkshakeFlavors()` method from the milkshake object. If the object was in a plural form, the method created would be `getMilkshakeFlavorss()`.

The schema itself is straightforward, but there are a few small options we should quickly go over:

- `package="lib.model"`

  When Symfony will generate our models, they will be placed inside the `lib/model` folder. Later when we take a look at plugins, you will see that this can be changed.

- `onDelete="CASCADE"`

  By default, Symfony enforces referential integrity by using the RESTRICT value for the `onDelete` attribute. This means that if we wanted to delete a milkshake, the system would prevent that as the milkshake is associated with flavors. Therefore, using the CASCADE value will allow us to delete the item.

 Further information about this is available on the Propel web site `http://propel.phpdb.org/trac/wiki/Users/Documentation/1.3/Relationships`.

- `phpName="MilkShake"`

  Although this attribute can be omitted, it gives us the ability to name the generated models. Although Symfony will do this automatically, this adds flexibility.

- `required="true"`

  The `required` attribute can be set to either `true` or `false`. This will either mean the field has to contain data or it doesn't have to. If this attribute is set to `true` when using the admin generator, the generated form will be in bold.

Symfony offers special handling of date/time fields. The fields must be named `created_at` or `created_on`, `updated_at` or `updated_on`. When first saving a record, if you have a field named `created_at`, Symfony will transparently add in the data/time. This also goes for the `updated_at` field.

We have created the database schema. Next, before using Symfony's CLI task, we must set up the database connections to build our database tables and the corresponding models, forms, and filters.

Configuring the ORM layer

The earlier versions of Symfony included the Propel ORM library as a part of its core components. But with releases of the new versions, it was decided to move the ORM out from its core framework and package the ORM as a plugin. The reason behind this is Doctrine, which is the other popular ORM used with Symfony. The new releases now allow the developer to easily choose which ORM they prefer. Both ORMs are packaged as plugins and are distributed with Symfony. Although Doctrine is now the default ORM, our application will be using Propel. However, later we'll be looking at a plugin that allows you to interchange ORMs.

As mentioned previously, the first file that Symfony reads is the `ProjectConfiguration.class.php` file, which is where we set configuration options for our project. It's located in our project's `config` folder. For example, we can enable plugins and set default folders. Now let's modify the `ProjectConfiguration.class.php` file from the `config` folder after making the change:

```php
<?php

require_once dirname(__FILE__).'/../lib/vendor/symfony/lib/autoload/
sfCoreAutoload.class.php';
sfCoreAutoload::register();

class ProjectConfiguration extends sfProjectConfiguration
{
  public function setup()
  {
    $this->enablePlugins('sfDoctrinePlugin');
  }
}
```

 Our configuration is what is included in the sandbox, if you have installed Symfony via PEAR then the path to the `sfCoreAutolad.class.php` will be different.

For us to enable Propel we have to change the plugin `sfDoctrinePlugin` to `sfPropelPlugin` like:

```php
<?php

require_once dirname(__FILE__).'/../lib/vendor/symfony/lib/autoload/
sfCoreAutoload.class.php';
sfCoreAutoload::register();

class ProjectConfiguration extends sfProjectConfiguration
{
  public function setup()
  {
    $this->enablePlugins('sfPropelPlugin');
  }
}
```

In Chapter 1, *Getting Started with Symfony*, I mentioned that Symfony uses autoloading to load all classes so that the developer does not need to use the `require()` function. The project configuration file is what starts this off, as you can see in the highlighted lines above. Also, you can see that our ORM plugin has been enabled. Every plugin that needs to be enabled needs to be defined here.

Configuring the database connection

In order to connect to our database, there are a few parameters that we need to set. These are the `username`, `password`, `host`, and the name of the database. All of these settings are defined in two configuration files — `databases.yml` and `propel.ini` — which again are located in the `config` folder with all other project-wide configuration files.

Setting these parameters can be done either by using a Symfony task on the CLI or by directly editing the files. Let's add them via the command line as follows:

```
$/home/timmy/workspace/milkshake>symfony configure:database
                "mysql:host=localhost;dbname=milkshake" root myPassword
```

After executing the above task, open both `databases.yml` and `propel.ini` files. In them you will see that the database connection properties have now been updated.

Opening both of the database configuration files and entering the details manually is preferred because then you don't have to remember the tasks' parameters. Also, from a security point of view you should never enter a password directly on the command line where the password is in plain text.

Using another database engine

By default, Symfony is configured to use the MySQL database. Of course, Symfony supports many other databases such as PostgreSQL, Oracle, SQLite, and MSSQL. Just to show you how easy it is to change to another database, I will set up my project for use with PostgreSQL. This is included here only as an example to demonstrate how to change database engines. For our application, we will be using MySQL.

In the `database.yml` file, you will see the following:

```
all:
  propel:
    class: sfPropelDatabase
    param:
      classname: PropelPDO
      dsn: 'pgsql:host=localhost;dbname=milkshake'
      username: root
      password: myPassword
      encoding: utf8
      persistent: true
      pooling: true
```

In the `propel.ini` file, you will see the following:

```
propel.database          = pgsql
propel.database.driver   = pgsql
propel.database.url      = pgsql:host=localhost;dbname=milkshake
```

Generating the models, forms, and filters

The Symfony tasks handle building all of the models, forms, and filters. When we were creating the database schema earlier, I mentioned that the schema is the root of all models, forms, and filters. To show this in action, we are going to generate them all. When you execute the tasks, the `schema.xml` file is parsed and then the ORM layer is generated based on it. At your terminal, execute the following three tasks:

```
$/home/timmy/workspace/milkshake>symfony propel:build-model

$/home/timmy/workspace/milkshake>symfony propel:build-forms

$/home/timmy/workspace/milkshake>symfony propel:build-filters
```

Now we have generated the entire ORM layer and all the generated classes are located in your `lib` folder. If you take a look inside the `lib` folder, you will see that there are three new subfolders— `form`, `filter`, and `model` —which all contain the classes. In Chapter 3, *Adding the Business Logic and Complex Application Logic*, we will take a look at these generated classes.

In the following screenshot, you can see the overall folder structure:

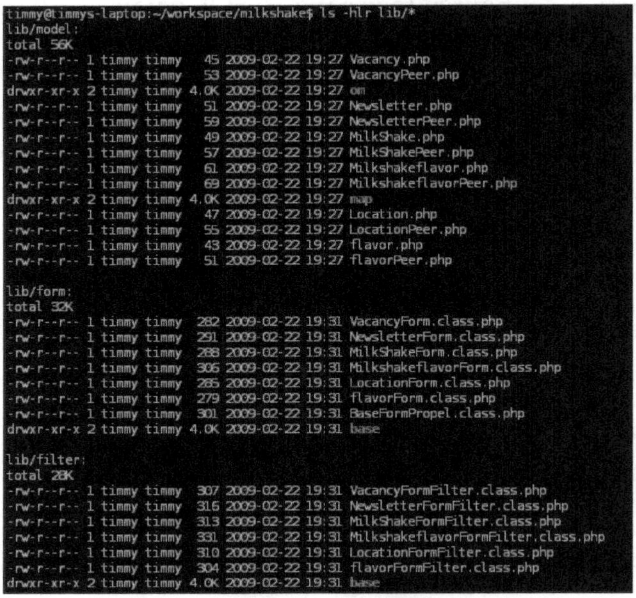

Building the database

The last step is to create the database and then create all of the tables. I have created my database called `milkshake` on the CLI using the following command:

```
$/home/timmy/workspace/milkshake>mysqladmin create milkshake -u root -p
```

Now that we have created the database, we need to generate the SQL that will create our tables. Again, we are going to use a Symfony task for this. Just like creating the ORM layer, the task will build the SQL based on the `schema.xml` file. From the CLI, execute the following task:

```
$/home/timmy/workspace/milkshake>symfony propel:build-sql
```

This has now generated a SQL file that contains all of the SQL statements needed to build the tables in our database. This file is located in the `data/sql` folder within the project folder. Looking at the generated `lib.model.schema.sql` file in this folder, you can view the SQL. Next, we need to insert the SQL into the database. Again using a Symfony task, execute the following on the CLI:

```
$/home/timmy/workspace/milkshake>symfony propel:insert-sql
```

During the execution of the task, you will be prompted to enter a *y* or *N* as to whether you want to delete the existing data. As this command will delete your existing tables and then create new tables, enter *y*. During development, the confirmation can become tiring. To get around this you can append the `no-confirmation` switch to the end as shown here:

```
>symfony propel:insert-sql --no-confirmation
```

Afterwards, check in your database and you should see all of the tables created as shown in the following screenshot:

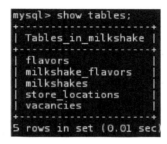

```
mysql> show tables;
+---------------------+
| Tables_in_milkshake |
+---------------------+
| flavors             |
| milkshake_flavors   |
| milkshakes          |
| store_locations     |
| vacancies           |
+---------------------+
5 rows in set (0.01 sec)
```

I have showed you how to execute each of the tasks in order to build everything. But there is a simpler way to do this, and that is with yet another Symfony task which executes all of the above tasks:

```
$/home/timmy/workspace/milkshake>symfony propel:build-all
```

or

```
$/home/timmy/workspace/milkshake>symfony propel:build-all --no-
confirmation
```

Our application is now all set up with a database and the ORM layer configured. Next, we can start on the application logic and produce a wireframe.

Creating the application modules

In Symfony, all requests are initially handled by a front controller before being passed to an action. The actions then implement the application logic before returning the presentation template that will be rendered.

Our application will initially contain four areas — home, `location`, menu, and `vacancies`. These areas will essentially form **modules** within our frontend application. A module is similar to an application, which is the place to group all application logic and is self contained. Let's now create the modules on the CLI by executing the following tasks:

```
$/home/timmy/workspace/milkshake>symfony generate:module frontend home

$/home/timmy/workspace/milkshake>symfony generate:module frontend
                                                        location

$/home/timmy/workspace/milkshake>symfony generate:module frontend menu

$/home/timmy/workspace/milkshake>symfony generate:module frontend
                                                        vacancies
```

Executing these tasks will create all of the modules' folder structures along with default actions, templates, and tests in our `frontend` application. You will see the following screenshot when running the first task:

```
timmy@timmys-laptop:~/workspace/milkshake$ symfony generate:module frontend home
>> dir+        /home/timmy/workspace/milkshake...s/frontend/modules/home/actions
>> file+       /home/timmy/workspace/milkshake.../home/actions/actions.class.php
>> dir+        /home/timmy/workspace/milkshake...frontend/modules/home/templates
>> file+       /home/timmy/workspace/milkshake...home/templates/indexSuccess.php
>> file+       /home/timmy/workspace/milkshake...al/frontend/homeActionsTest.php
>> tokens      /home/timmy/workspace/milkshake...al/frontend/homeActionsTest.php
>> tokens      /home/timmy/workspace/milkshake.../home/actions/actions.class.php
>> tokens      /home/timmy/workspace/milkshake...home/templates/indexSuccess.php
```

Let's examine the folder structure for a module:

Folder	Description
actions	This folder contains the actions class and components class for a module
templates	All modules templates are stored in this folder

Now browse to `http://milkshake/frontend_dev.php/menu` and you will see Symfony's default page for our `menu` module. Notice that this page also provides useful information on what to do next. This information, of course, is to render our template rather than have Symfony forward the request.

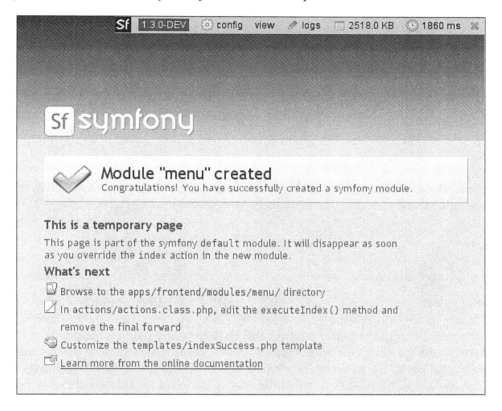

Handling the routing

We have just tested our menu module and Symfony was able to handle this request without us having to set anything. This is because the URL was interpreted as `http://milkshake/module/action/:params`. If the action is missing, Symfony will automatically append `index` and execute the `index` action if one exists in the module. Looking at the URL for our `menu` module, we can use either `http://milkshake/frontend_dev.php/menu` or `http://milkshake/frontend_dev.php/menu/index` for the moment. Also, if you want to pass variables from the URL, then we can just add them to the end of the URL. For example, if we wanted to also pass `page=1` to the `menu` module, the URL would be `http://milkshake/frontend_dev.php/menu/index/page/1`. The problem here is that we must also specify the name of the action, which doesn't leave much room for customizing a URL.

Mapping the URL to the application logic is called **routing**. In the earlier example, we browsed to `http://milkshake/frontend_dev.php/menu` and Symfony was able to route that to our `menu` module without us having to configure anything. First, let's take a look at the routing file located at `apps/frontend/config/routing.yml`.

```
# default rules
homepage:
  URL:    /
  param: { module: default, action: index }
default_index:
  URL:    /:module
  param: { action: index }
default:
  URL:    /:module/:action/*
```

This is the default routing file that was generated for us. Using the home page routing rules as an example, the route is broken down into three parts:

- A unique label: `homepage`
- A URL pattern: `URL: /`
- An array of request parameters: `param: { module: menu, action: index }`

We refer to each one of the rules within the routing file using a unique label. A URL pattern is what Symfony uses to map the URL to a rule, and the array of parameters is what maps the request to the module and the action. By using a routing file, Symfony caters for complicated URLs, which can restrict parameter types, request methods, and associate parameters to our Propel ORM layer. In fact, Symfony includes an entire framework that handles the routing for us. In the later chapters, we will expand on routing.

The application logic

As we have seen, Symfony routes all requests to an action within a module. So let's open the `actions` class for our `menu` module, which is located at `apps/frontend/modules/menu/actions/actions.class.php`.

```php
class menuActions extends sfActions
{
 /**
  * Executes index action
  *
  * @param sfRequest $request A request object
  */
```

```
    public function executeIndex(sfWebRequest $request)
    {
      $this->forward('default', 'module');
    }
  }
```

This `menuActions` class contains all of the menu actions and as you can see, it extends the `sfActions` base class. This class was generated for us along with a default 'index' action (method). The default index action simply forwards the request to Symfony's default module, which in turn generates the default page that we were presented with.

All of the actions follow the same naming convention, that is, the action name must begin with the word `execute` followed by the action name starting with a capital letter. Also, the request object is passed to the action, which contains all of the parameters that are in the request.

Let's begin by modifying the default behavior of the `menu` module to display our own template. Here we need the application logic to return the template name that needs to be rendered. To do this, we simply replace the call to the `forward` function with a `return` statement that has the template name:

```
    public function executeIndex(sfWebRequest $request)
    {
      return sfView::SUCCESS;
    }
```

A default index template was also generated for us in the `templates` folder, that is, `apps/frontend/modules/menu/templates/indexSuccess.php`. Returning the `sfView::SUCCESS` constant will render this template for us. The template rendered will depend on the returned string from the action. All templates must also follow the naming convention of `actionNameReturnString.php`. Therefore, our action called `index` returns the `sfView` constant `SUCCESS`, meaning that the `indexSuccess.php` template needs to be present within the `templates` folder for our `menu` module. We can return other strings, such as these:

- `return sfView::ERROR`: Looks for the `indexError.php` template
- `return myTemplate`: Looks for the `indexmyTemplate.php` template
- `return sfView::NONE`: Will not return a template and, therefore, bypass the view layer; this could be used as an example for an AJAX request

However, just removing the `$this->forward('default', 'module')` function will also return `indexSuccess.php` by default. It is worth adding the return value for ease in reading. Now that we have rendered the `menu` template, go ahead and do the same for the `home`, `locations`, and `vacancies` modules.

Rendering the template

The final step is to create the needed XHTML to render the template. **Views** (or **templates** as they are known) form the presentation layer. Although I am discussing a template as one whole entity, it is not entirely true. Just like all good template frameworks (Smarty, for example), a template can consist of reusable components. As with Symfony, there is no exception. We will be exploring these in greater detail in later chapters.

In a nutshell, as the template is rendered, it pulls in all other modules as they are called (with the exception of *slots*) and then decorates the template with a wrapper *layout* template.

 Although developers are free to use PHP code in the templates, PHP should be kept to an absolute minimum, and serve only for presentation logic.

There are two folders where we can keep templates—the `moduleName/templates` folder or the `apps/templates` folder. The former holds all templates for your module and the latter is where all your global templates reside. If you look inside the global template folder, you will see the global layout template—`layout.php`. This global template contains all of the code for the outer shell of the module template. This wrapper template is where we have things such as the HTML starting tags, meta tags, title tags, and others, along with the main XHTML closing tags.

Let's look at the main layout template in `apps/frontend/templates/layout.php`:

```
<!DOCTYPE html PUBLIC "-//W3C//DTD XHTML 1.0 Transitional//EN"
        "http://www.w3.org/TR/xhtml1/DTD/xhtml1-transitional.dtd">

<html xmlns="http://www.w3.org/1999/xhtml" xml:lang="en" lang="en">
  <head>
    <?php include_http_metas() ?>
    <?php include_metas() ?>
    <?php include_title() ?>
    <link rel="shortcut icon" href="/favicon.ico" />
    <?php include_stylesheets() ?>
    <?php include_javascripts() ?>
  </head>
  <body>
    <?php echo $sf_content ?>
  </body>
</html>
```

It is worth noting how the meta tags and title tags are included in the first part of the template. These are all passed in either from a view configuration file or by the action as follows:

```php
<?php include_http_metas() ?>
<?php include_metas() ?>
<?php include_title() ?>
```

The second part is how our module template is included in the global template. In this case, the layout template is rending the raw format of the generated module template. Symfony has a few escaping settings, meaning that it will turn certain characters into their HTML equivalents.

As this layout is a part of the overall template and, therefore, generally present as part of all templates, we are going to add the navigation to this template. But before we do so, we need to add our routing rules so that we can add the navigation links.

Adding our routing rules

At the moment, Symfony is able to find our pages by `module/action` and because we use the default index action, Symfony will render our template. Now we need to add links to our application. We could just create the links that point to `module/action`, but this will soon get complicated as the site scales upwards. Besides, there is also a production and development controller involved. So instead of just creating links, we will create the routing rules. Our links will reference the routing rules and, therefore, will generate the URLs for us. Open up the `routing.yml` file in the `apps/frontend/config` folder and add the following:

```yaml
# default rules
homepage:
  URL:    /
  param: { module: default, action: index }

menu:
  URL:    /menu
  param: { module: menu, action: index }

locations:
  URL:    /locations
  param: { module: location, action: index }

vacancies:
  URL:    /vacancies
  param: { module: vacancies, action: index }

default_index:
```

```
  URL:    /:module
  param: { action: index }
default:
  URL:    /:module/:action/*
```

As you can see, we have followed the same pattern as the default rules. We first added a label and then defined the URL pattern, followed by the module and action. Now let's go back to our layout template.

 Make sure your rules are above the `default` and `default_index` rules.

To access these routes from within, the template Symfony provides these helpers—`link_to()` and `url_for()`. Essentially, a helper is a function that returns HTML. In the case of these two helpers, they will return an HTML link tag. We are going to add the following four links to our layout:

```php
<?php echo link_to('Home', '@home') ?>
<?php echo link_to('Menu', '@menu') ?>
<?php echo link_to('Store Locations', '@locations
<?php echo link_to('Vacancies', '@vacancies
```

The first parameter passed to the helper is the text that will be displayed as the link. The second parameter references a rule in the routing; we simply start with the @ symbol followed by the routing label. When you look at the final page a little later, you will see that Symfony has correctly inserted the URL for us. Depending on what controller we are using, the correct controller will also be inserted as a part of the URL.

Configuring template parameters

We need to set the page titles in the HTML. As mentioned earlier, templates can be configured in a few ways. Here we are going to set the page title in the template configuration file. To do this, we must create a folder named `config` within each of the modules that we have already created, and create a `view.yml` file within the `config` folder. The `view.yml` configuration file will contain all of the meta and title descriptions, along with any other template-specific variables. There are many more options that we can set, but for now we will only need to set the basic settings. After you have created both the `config` folder and the `view.yml` file within the folder for the `menu` module, open your `view.yml` file and add the following:

```
indexSuccess:
  metas:
    title:        Our Menu
```

The first parameter references the template by the file name. Our template is `indexSuccess.php` and so we use the filename minus the extension. Now we would like to set the page title within the metas. This file can now be copied to all the other `config` folders that you have created; of course, you just have to amend the title. Being able to configure all templates within a module forces a tightly coded application. This file is great if we don't need the title to be dynamic, but we will address that later.

After copying this file to all the other modules and changing the titles, you are all done!

Styling the pages

The last step is to add a little CSS to give the pages an initial wireframe feeling. On my layout template, I have added the inline styling which sets the page up.

This is the `layout.php` template. The highlighted lines indicate where I have added the final CSS:

```
<!DOCTYPE HTML PUBLIC "-//W3C//DTD XHTML 1.0 Transitional//EN"
            "http://www.w3.org/TR/xhtml1/DTD/xhtml1-transitional.dtd">

<HTML xmlns="http://www.w3.org/1999/xhtml" xml:lang="en" lang="en">

  <head>
    <?php include_http_metas() ?>
    <?php include_metas() ?>
    <?php include_title() ?>
    <link rel="shortcut icon" href="/favicon.ico" />
  <style type="text/css">
    body{margin:0; padding:0;
        font-family: Arial, Verdana, sans-serif;
        font-size: 11px;}
    a img,:link img,:visited img { border: none; color: #000000; }
  </style>
  </head>
  <body>
<div style="width: 786px; border: 1px solid #000000; margin: auto;">
<div style="height: 100px;">
    <div style="text-align: center"><h1>Top Banner</h1></div>
</div>

<div style="width: 192px; float: left; ">
    <div style="width: 100%; text-align: left;">
        <ul style="list-style-type:none;margin:0;padding:0;">
            <li style="margin:0;padding:0.25em 0.5em 0.25em 0.5em;
                width: 150px; border-bottom: 1px solid #000000;
                border-right: 1px solid #000000; ;
                border-top: 1px solid #000000; ">
```

```
            <?php echo link_to('Home', '@homepage') ?></li>
        <li style="margin:0;padding:0.25em 0.5em 0.25em 0.5em;
            width: 150px; border-bottom: 1px solid #000000;
            border-right: 1px solid #000000; ">
        <?php echo link_to('Menu', '@menu') ?></li>

        <li style="margin:0;padding:0.25em 0.5em 0.25em 0.5em;
            width: 150px; border-bottom: 1px solid #000000;
            border-right: 1px solid #000000;   ">
        <?php echo link_to('Store Locations', '@locations') ?></li>

        <li style="margin:0;padding:0.25em 0.5em 0.25em 0.5em;
            width: 150px; border-bottom: 1px solid #000000;
            border-right: 1px solid #000000;   ">
        <?php echo link_to('Vacancies', '@vacancies') ?></li>
      </ul>
    </div>
  </div>

  <div style="margin-left: 208px">
      <div style="min-height: 100px">
        <?php echo $sf_data->
        getRaw('sf_content') ?>
      </div>
  </div>

  <div style="text-align: center"><h1>Footer</h1></div>
  <div style="clear:both"></div>
  </div>
  </body>
  </html>
```

With the result HTML added to our layout, we now get a nice wire frame that resembles the site:

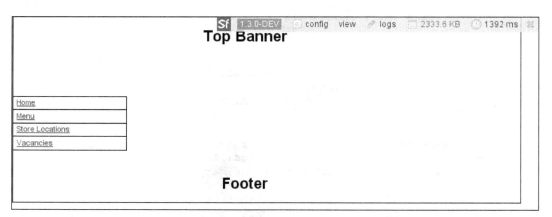

Debugging:

When developing and trying to troubleshoot, it is important to use the `frontend_dev.php` controller. Otherwise, the errors will not be revealed as Symfony hides them in a production environment.

Using the development controller means we can use the debug bar at the top of the window to see what is happening. Also, there are log files available to us in the log folder that can be used for troubleshooting.

Common installation problems

When first starting out, there are a few potential problems that you can encounter. Below are a few of the main errors that you might come across.

Web server 404 error page

The requested URL `/index.php` file was not found on this server.

This is because you haven't created an application. So, on the command line enter:

```
>symfony app frontend
```

This will create the application, along with the controllers, `index.php` and `frontend_dev.php`.

A symfony 'Oop! An error occurred'

One thing to remember is this page is in fact the default Symfony 500 error page, and not a web server 500 error page. While developing, you should always use the development controller (`app_dev.php`). The development controller lets you see the exact problem. The production controller (`index.php`) hides the problem away from the users.

Pages and debug bar do not render correctly

Another common problem is that when you configure your virtual hosts, you will often leave an important line out and therefore will be left seeing a page with no CSS.

```
symfony PHP Framework
ok
```

Symfony Project Created

Congratulations! You have successfully created your symfony project.

Project setup successful
    This project uses the symfony libraries. If you see no image in this page, you may need to configure your web server so that it gains access to the symfony_data/web/sf/ directory.
This is a temporary page
    This page is part of the symfony default module. It will disappear as soon as you define a homepage route in your routing.yml.
What's next
  • Create your data model
  • Customize the layout of the generated templates
  • Learn more from the online documentation

Sf
• 1.0.14
• Config vars & config
• Comment logs & msgs
• Memory 3667.7 KB
• Time 73 ms
  Close

As you can see the above page has lost all CSS styling. This is caused by not including an alias directive in you virtual host configuration file. Include the following in virtual host configuration file:

```
#Set symfony alias
Alias /sf /usr/share/php/data/symfony/web/sf
```

On some Linux installations, you need to also include:

```
<Directory "/usr/share/php/data/symfony/web/sf ">
    Allow from all
</Directory >
```

Throughout the book we are going to learn the ins and outs of Symfony and in no time at all will know why Symfony truly is an excellent framework.

Summary

By using Symfony's CLI to create a project, a developer can spend more time coding. Also, the initial overview of the controllers, routing, application logic, applications, and modules show how tight and modular Symfony can be to develop with. This enforces that developers adhere to standards that make refactoring, debugging, and extending others' code easy. Also, it helps developers to code in an agile way.

We have so far covered the basics that have allowed us to get a *wireframe* version of our milkshake application up and ready. We have used some of the Symfony tasks to generate the majority of files and code, and have added a few little tweaks to get the pages linking and working. Also, we have configured the framework to use the Propel plugin and have the database ready for the next chapter.

3
Adding the Business Logic and Complex Application Logic

In the previous chapter we generated the project and modules, built our database, generated the ORM layer, and created a working wireframe of our milkshake application. Now, we can start to generate a working prototype that uses the database.

By the end of this chapter, you will learn how to:

- Pre-populate the database with test data using Propel
- Create business logic within the ORM
- Use an ORM to increase productivity
- Create more complex routing rules
- Download and install a plugin
- Separate chunks of template code into partials

The generated models

Although we have only created five tables, looking in the `lib/model` folder, and the subfolders of `om/` and `map/` reveals that there are a total of 25 files. The files that we are interested in are located in the `lib/model` and `lib/model/om` folders. The files generated in the `lib/model/om` folder contain all of the *base* classes, and the files in the `lib/model` folder contain the *custom* classes that extend the base classes.

You will also notice that for each class there is also a corresponding *peer* class. The peer classes are what we use to query the database, and are referred to as the **Data Access Objects (DAOs)**. Within these classes, there are numerous methods created for us. The non-peer counterpart represents the rows of the table in the result set and provides us with methods to access the data in each row.

The custom classes are where we add our methods to query the database. It is important that we add all our code to the custom classes, and if need be extend the base classes functions here too. The reason for this is if a change is made to the schema when we use the Symfony task to rebuild the models, all of the base classes will be regenerated. The custom models remain untouched.

 Although we have used the Symfony task earlier to create these files, this has all been handled via the Propel ORM library.

Populating the database

As mentioned above, throughout an application's development cycle, changes to the database will be inevitable sooner or later. This means that changes to your schema will result in the rebuilding of the models, forms, and filters as well as the deletion and recreation of the database tables. If you already have a pre-populated database, it makes no sense to manually re-enter all the data. Of course, you could create an SQL patch file, but Symfony helps to make this process less of a headache by a fixtures YAML file.

A **fixtures** file allows a developer to add test data, which is used to populate the database. On the command line, you can use a Symfony task that will insert this data for you. To insert the data, the models that we created earlier are used. This mimics the same process that we will use to retrieve and insert our own data.

As a part of the project creation process, a fixtures file — fixtures.yml — was generated in the data/fixtures folder and contains an example. Open this file, delete its content, and replace with our data as follows:

```
MilkShake:
  m1:
    name: Blueberry
    calories: 200
    image_url: blueberry.jpg
  m2:
    name: Chocolate Digestive
    calories: 400
    image_url: chocolate_digestive.jpg
  m3:
    name: Raspberry
    calories: 250
    image_url: raspberry.jpg
Flavor:
  f1:
```

```
      name: Banana
    f2:
      name: Strawberry
    f3:
      name: Cheesecake
    f4:
      name: Chocolate

  MilkshakeFlavor:
    mf1:
      milkshake_id:   m1
      flavor_id:      f15
    mf2:
      milkshake_id:   m2
      flavor_id:      f10
    mf3:
      milkshake_id:   m3
      flavor_id:      f13
    mf4:
      milkshake_id:   m6
      flavor_id:      f1
    mf5:
      milkshake_id:   m6
      flavor_id:      f2
  StoreLocation:
    l1:
      address1: The Strand
      address2:
      postcode: wc2r we4
      country: uk
      phone: +44 (0)208 789 9875
      fax: +44 (0)208 789 9876
```

The structure of the file is pretty straightforward. The labels represent the classes of each of the tables. Looking at the StoreLocation label, we have a corresponding StoreLocation class that represents the store_locations table. The l1 key represents that record as a unique object, which allows us to reference if needed as we have done in the MilkshakesFlavor section. The final attributes are the attributes of the class that represent the table columns.

Now we have test data, and can use the Symfony task to insert it for us. Enter the following Symfony task in your terminal window:

```
$/home/timmy/workspace/milkshake>symfony propel:data-load
```

Now that we have a populated database, we can start the process of introducing the business logic to our site.

It is important to note that the YAML syntax does not accept tabs, but only spaces. Also, correct indentation is required. Visit their web site at `http://www.yaml.org/` to get a grips on YAML.

Your IDE should allow you to use spaces rather than a tab.

Retrieving data using the models

We will start by implementing the menu page. The initial functionality of the menu page will be to retrieve a list of all the milkshakes in alphabetical order.

Defining the criteria

To retrieve a result set, we have to initialize a `Criteria` object and customize it. This object then represents an SQL query. As our custom classes extend the base class, we use one of a number of methods of the parent. Passing the `Criteria` object to the method results in the query that is performed on our database. The `Criteria` object can handle both simple and relatively complicated queries. However, as a rule it is a good practice to customize the `Criteria` object to only retrieve what you want. This will be covered in detail in Chapter 9, *Optimizing for performance*.

Opening the `lib/model/MilkShakePeer.php` file reveals that there are no methods. As this is a custom class, it is up to us to add our business logic. Here we need to create a static method to retrieve data about all the milkshakes from the database in alphabetical order. Let's begin by adding a `getAllShakes()` method, which I have done in the following code snippet:

```
/**
 * Get all of the milkshakes
 *
 * @param Int $limit total amount to be returned. 0 = unlimited
 * @return Array Array containing objects
 */
public static function getAllShakes($limit=0)
{
  //Create the criteria
  $c = new Criteria();

  //Set the limit
  if(0 > $limit)
  {
    $c->setLimit($limit);
  }

  //Order by name in ascending order
```

```
    $c->addAscendingOrderByColumn(self::NAME);

    return self::doSelect($c);
}
```

In this code snippet, we first instantiate the `Criteria` object and then customize the criteria by setting a limit, if one is required, using the `setLimit()` method. This translates into the SQL `Limit` clause. To set an `order by` clause, we need to use the `Criteria` object's `addAscendingOrderByColumn()` method. This method takes the column name with which we want to order the result set as an argument. That's all we need to do to the `Criteria` object. Next, we call the `doSelect()` parent method and pass it to our `Criteria` object.

Hydration

The `doSelect()` method does more than just querying the database. After this function has been called, the results are returned to the method and then the results are converted into our model objects. The whole process is called **hydration**. Essentially, the following happens in the hydrating process:

1. An SQL query is created and optimized for our chosen database.
2. All values that we pass to the `Criteria` object are escaped and are safe to use.
3. The database is queried.
4. A result set is returned as an array of objects.

This is a very quick and convenient way of retrieving our data. However, with ease comes danger. It is very easy to fall into the habit of retrieving everything even if we only need one or two columns. We'll look at bypassing the hydration process in Chapter 9, *Optimizing for Performance*.

Autoloading

You may have noticed that there are no PHP `include()` or `require()` functions. This is because Symfony implements class `Autoloading`. When you first run your application, Symfony registers all the classes, compiles an associative array, and stores it in cache so that it doesn't have to repeat the process. Therefore, when adding new classes, we have to clear the Symfony cache. We will learn to clear the Symfony cache later in this chapter, after installing a plugin.

All our column titles are class constants, so refer to the column as `self::COL_NAME`.

Retrieving the result set from the action

In Chapter 2, *Developing Our Application*, we briefly looked at the application logic in the `actions` class. We have now looked at the business logic—creating a custom query, calling this function, and then passing the results to the template so that we can display the information. Going back into the `menuAction` class in `apps/frontend/modules/menu/actions/actions.class.php`, append the index action with the following:

```
/**
 * Executes index action
 *
 */
public function executeIndex()
{
    //Get all out all of the shakes
    $this->milkshakeArray = MilkShakePeer::getAllShakes();

    return sfView::SUCCESS;
}
```

Looking at this code snippet, we make a call to our `MilkShakePeer` model and use our static function `getAllShakes()`. As all the peer functions provide static methods, we use the scope resolution operator (`::`) to access our static function.

When giving the template access to variables, you must use `$this` as Symfony uses PHP magic functions widely. Assigning variables with the `$this->milkshakeArray = value` results in calling of the `sfAction` method, which assigns the variable to the view variables.

To see what variables are available to the template, we can also look at the web debug bar. If you browse to the menu page `http://milkshake/frontend_dev.php/menu` and click on the **view** link, you will see that there is an array parameter called `$milkshakeArray`. The (array) part of the variable is of the `variable` type. If we set two other variables in my action `this->test = 1` and `$this->test2 = true`, we will get the following output:

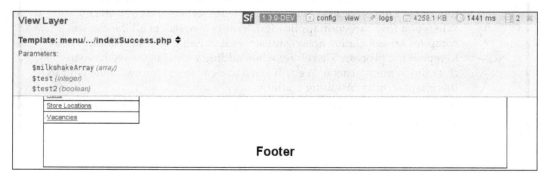

The template logic

The index action has created a variable that can be accessed from the template. We can access the variable from the template by calling $milkshakeArray. Before displaying the results, let's take a look at what exactly is returned from the ORM and how we can use the DAOs to access the rows within the result set.

Returned results

Our results are returned as an array of objects. If we were to call print_r($milkshakeArray) on the template or in the action, you would see the following:

```
Array
(
    [0] => MilkShake Object
        (
            [id:protected] => 26
            [name:protected] => Blackberry
            [image_url:protected] => blackberry.jpg
            [thumb_url:protected] =>
            [calories:protected] => 400
            [created_at:protected] => 1213300967
            [updated_at:protected] => 1213300967
            [collMilkshakeFlavours:protected] =>
            [lastMilkshakeFlavourCriteria:protected] =>
            [alreadyInSave:protected] =>
            [alreadyInValidation:protected] =>
            [validationFailures:protected] => Array
                (
                )

            [_new:private] =>
            [_deleted:private] =>
            [modifiedColumns:protected] => Array
                (
                )

        )

    [1] => MilkShake Object
        (
            [id:protected] => 19
            [name:protected] => Blueberry
            [image_url:protected] => blueberry.jpg
            [thumb_url:protected] =>
            [calories:protected] => 200
```

```
[created_at:protected] => 1213300967
[updated_at:protected] => 1213300967
[collMilkshakeFlavours:protected] =>
[lastMilkshakeFlavourCriteria:protected] =>
[alreadyInSave:protected] =>
[alreadyInValidation:protected] =>
[validationFailures:protected] => Array
    (
    )

[_new:private] =>
[_deleted:private] =>
[modifiedColumns:protected] => Array
    (
    )
)
```

Each row of the results has been converted to an associative array, along with all the columns and a few more extra parts, which we will look at later. However, the columns cannot be accessed directly from the array as the results are in fact objects. Therefore, we must use the DAO class.

Using the DAOs

The DAO allows us to retrieve each of the columns from the results in a very easy and convenient way through access methods. In relation to the column names in our milkshakes table, for example, we have a column named image_url and you can see that it is also present in the returned results. The getter methods for this column are slightly different because of the transition from a table to an object. Therefore, the ORM layer has generated a getImageUrl() method for accessing the data in this column. It has stripped out the underscores and replaced the next section of the name with a capital letter. This naming convention is the same for all the columns.

Displaying the results

With all this in mind, we can go ahead and add the following to the indexSuccess. php templates in the apps/frontend/modules/menu/templates folder:

```php
<?php $i=0 ?>

<?php foreach($milkshakeArray as $milkshake): ?>

    <div style="width: 176px; float: left; padding-bottom: 20px;
```

```
            margin-right: 16px; margin-bottom: 16px;">
        <div style="height: 250px; ">
            <?php echo image_tag('/images/'.$milkshake->getImageUrl(),
                            array('alt'=>$milkshake->getName())); ?>
        </div>
        <div>
          Name:<?php echo link_to($milkshake->getName(), 'menu_item',
                            $milkshake) ?><br />
          Calories: <?php echo $milkshake->getCalories() ?>
        </div>
    </div>

    <?php if(($i%3) == 2):  ?>
        <div style="clear:both"></div>
    <?php endif ?>

  <?php $i++ ?>
<?php endforeach; ?>
```

The first thing we can look at is the loop. Note the colon at the end of the `for()` declaration:

```
<?php foreach($milkshakeArray as $milkshake ): ?>
    . . .
<?php endfor; ?>
```

All loops and `if` statements should end with a colon (`:`) and terminate with an `end` statement. Although it is not compulsory, it makes the template code more uniform. Not to mention, the Eclipse PDT plugin caters for this.

Each row is accessed through the object's getter methods. For example, we are able to access the `name`, `image_url`, and `calories` columns with their appropriate getter methods:

```
echo $milkshake->getImageUrl();
echo $milkshake->getName();
echo $milkshake->getCalories();
```

Helpers

The last thing to note is the use of the `link_to()` and `image_tag()` helpers. Symfony provides HTML helpers. A **helper** is a reusable PHP function that simply returns code, such as HTML and Javascript. We used the `link_to()` helper in the previous chapter to add the navigation. Using helpers can not only speed up development time, but also can make code more readable and reusable. To use a helper(s), we need to declare it in the template by adding:

```
use_helper('helper1', 'helper2')
```

This code allows the template to use `helper1` and `helper2` along with the other default helpers, which are included as part of Symfony.

Of course, the default helpers that are loaded can be configured in the `settings.yml` file. Although they do appear to be commented out, the values in the comments are the default values. As we progress with the site, you will learn how to use all of the popular helpers.

In our template we use the `image_tag()` helper, which is one of the many helper functions.

```php
<?php echo image_tag('/images/milkshake_images/'
                        .$milkshakeArray[$i]->getImageUrl()); ?>
```

Looking at the XHTML source, you can see that this snippet outputs as the `<img>` tag. Although we have not specified the `img` tag's `alt` attribute, Symfony has done this for us by using the image name.

```
<img src="/images/milkshake_images/blueberry.jpg" alt="Blueberry" />
```

But we can modify the other attributes. For example, use the following in our database if we have an `image_alt_tag` column:

```php
<?php echo image_tag('/uploads/assets/milkshake_images/'
                .$milkshakeArray[$i]->getImageUrl(),
                'alt="'.$milkshakeArray[$i]->getImageAltTag()
                .'" style="border:1px solid #000"'); ?>
```

Alternatively, if you wanted to use the `image_tag()` helper on a page, you can pass in other parameters. The following is an example:

```php
image_tag('/images/myimage.jpg', array('alt'=>'My Image',
                                    'class'=>'cssClass'))
```

After everything is saved, you can go ahead and click on the **Menu** link in the navigation. This will give you the following screenshot:

Now that we have the menu, there are two other things we need to look at:

- We have only added nine milkshakes. What if our menu grows to 100 or more?
- We should provide a page for every milkshake, so that we can display other information to the user.

The first thing we will look at is dealing with a much larger result set. Using the Propel pager is the solution, as this introduces pagination to our result set.

Paginating our menu

Introducing pagination only requires a few minor adjustments in our code. Also, to make the pagination configurable, we are going to add a few application parameters, which we can set rather than hardcoding.

Adding the pager business logic

The first step involves modifying our `getAllShakes()` method in the `MilkShakePeer` model. The Propel ORM has a pager object that simplifies the process for us. In `lib/model/MilkShakePeer.php`, let's create the pager object.

```
public static function getAllShakes($currentPage, $totalItems)
{
    //Create the criteria
    $c = new Criteria();

    //Order by name in ascending order
    $c->addAscendingOrderByColumn(self::NAME);

    //Create the pager object
        $pagerObj = new sfPropelPager('MilkShake', $totalItems);
        $pagerObj->setCriteria($c);
        $pagerObj->setPage($currentPage);
        $pagerObj->init();

    return $pagerObj;

}
```

We use the `sfPropelPager()` object, which takes the result object and the total price of each items that we wish to see on each page. We then pass in the same `Criteria` object and set the current page.

Setting a configuration option

At the moment, there is no requirement for a user to set the total amount of items that can be viewed at a time. Also, during the development stage you might want to show a prototype with six or nine items. Setting a variable in the class is usually preferred.

One feature which is extremely useful in Symfony is the configuration files. In our frontend application, you might have noticed a file named `app.yml` within the `app/frontend/config/` folder. All global application-specific variables are specified in this configuration file. In this file, we will create a parameter to hold the total amount of items that we want displayed. For example, we could add the following to the `apps/frontend/config/app.yml` file:

```
# default values
all:
  total_menu_items:    6
```

All configuration files in Symfony can be accessed by both templates and actions through the `sfConfig` static class, provided they reside in the global `app.yml` file.

However, if you want to set values on a module level, this can be accomplished in the same manner. As the pagination variables are only required in our menu module, we will create a folder named `config/`. Inside that folder we will create a `module.yml` file where we can insert our attributes and values. We have already created a `config/` folder in the previous chapter, so let's go ahead and create a file named `module.yml` in there and add this:

```
# default values
all:
  total_menu_items:    6
```

Amending the action

There are a few minor changes to make and a little refactoring to do in the action in order to finish off the pagination. The main change is passing the correct arguments into the `getAllShakes()` method that we just amended. One parameter will be a part of the request and the other comes from the configuration file that we just amended.

Accessing the $_POST, $_GET, and $_REQUEST variables

When a user clicks on our pagination, the best way to pass the page that the user wants to browse in your application is via the URL. In order to do this, we have to set up the routing, which is our next job. But for now, we are going to say that we wish to store the page in a variable that is called `page`.

Symfony's parameter holders means that we do not use `$_GET`, `$_POST`, or `$_REQUEST` anymore. Instead, we use `$request->getParameter('var')`. Why we stick to retrieving the variables through Symfony is because Symfony cleans the values for us and thus makes them safe to use.

We can access the `page` variable in the action by the `getParameter()` method of the `request` object like this:

```
$page = $request->getParameter('page');
```

This code is expecting to access the `page` variable. In some cases, it might not initially exist. To overcome this, we can set a default value in either the routing rules or pass in the default value to the function call. The following is an example:

```
$page = $request->getParameter('page', 1);
```

Accessing the application and module configuration file

Accessing a variable from the `module.yml` file within an action is straightforward. You just need to use the `sfConfig` class:

```
sfConfig::get('mod_menu_total_menu_items');
```

If this was set in the global `app.yml` file, you would use this:

```
sfConfig::get('app_total_menu_items');
```

These examples retrieve the `total_menu_items` variable from both the `module.yml` and the `app.yml` files. Notice the name of the variable begins with `mod_menu_` and `app_`. This references which configuration file the variable is set in. In our case, it references the module that the parameter is set for — menu.

Implementing this means we change the argument in our `action.class.php` to the following:

```
$this->milkshakeObj = MilkShakePeer::getAllShakes(
                          $request->getParameter('page'),
                          sfConfig::get('mod_menu_total_menu_items'));
```

As a part of refactoring, we are passing an object back to the template rather than passing an array. Therefore, I have changed the name of the variable to coincide with this.

Finally, we make sure that there are results in the database. Generally, this is not really a user's concern, but more of a developer concern. We should redirect the page to a 404 error page if there are no results in the database, and provide a useful log message number if we have forgotten to re-populate their locate database.

```
//Make sure there are results.
    $this->forward404If($this->milkshakeObj->getNbResults() < 1, 'No
Results in the Database');
```

If no results are returned, the user is forwarded to a 404 error page. Symfony offers three ways in which we can trigger a 404 error page:

- `$this->forward404(message)`
- `$this->forwad404If(condition, message)`
- `$this->forward404Unless(condition, message)`

Of course, we should really handle the event of no items in the database with another page. The full code for the action is as follows:

```
public function executeIndex(sfWebRequest $request)
  {
    //Get all out all of the shakes
    $this->milkshakeObj = MilkShakePeer::getAllShakes(
                    $request->getParameter('page'),
                  sfConfig::get('mod_menu_total_menu_items'));
    //Forward to 404 if no results
    $this->forward404If($this->milkshakeObj->getNbResults() < 1,
                    'No Results in the Database');
    return sfView::SUCCESS;
  }
```

Building up the routing

To include the new pagination, we have to modify the routing for the menu. We need to allow the page number to be included as part of the URL. In `apps/frontend/config/routing.yml`, change the `menu` label to the following:

```
menu:
  url:   /menu/:page
  class: sfRequestRoute
  param: { module: menu, action: index, page:1 }
  requirements:
    page: \d+
          sf_method: [get]
```

Going over the amended rule, I have appended /:page to the URL. This represents a variable named page, which will be included as part of the URL. This is enforced by using the sfRequestRoute class and the set of requirements. If the URL does not include a value for the page, it will default to 1. The requirements section can take regular expressions and really validate the variable in the URL.

 For larger projects, using requirements will help when you have similar rules.

Organizing a template with partials

Apart from the pagination on the template, we have everything else ready. As the logic to generate the pagination is going to contain many PHP tags, we should hide it. This will make the template a lot cleaner and easier to modify by others.

A **partial** returns HTML code and is reusable. So if we add other sections to our site that required paginated results, we could include the same partial on those pages and simply pass in to the partial the Propel pager object containing the results. The partial template can be located in one of three places:

- Globally
- Within the module that it is being used
- Within another module

If the partial is needed in more than one module, then it should be classified as global and should reside in the global templates folder — apps/frontend/templates. All templates have a naming convention, and this goes for partials too. The name of the partial must begin with an underscore as this helps it to be easily identifiable.

On our menu index page — indexSuccess.php — let's start by adding a include_partial statement underneath the endforeach closing tag.

```php
<?php include_partial('pagination',
                      array('paginationObj'=>$milkshakeObj)) ?>
```

By looking at this code, we can see that we are using another Symfony helper, include_partial(). This helper requires that we pass in the location/name of our partial. In our case, it will be located within the same template folder — apps/frontend/menu/templates. However, if it was global and other pages would use the partial, we would say that it's global:

```php
<?php include_partial('global/pagination',
                      array('paginationObj'=>$milkshakeObj)) ?>
```

Symfony knows where our partial is located and that it is called _pagination. php. The second argument can either be omitted or it can be data that the partial may need access to. Our pagination partial will require the Propel paging object to retrieve information about all the pages.

Onto the partial, let's create the partial by opening apps/frontend/modules/menu/ templates/_pagination.php and inserting the following:

```
<?php if ($paginationObj->haveToPaginate()): ?>
    <div style="margin-top: 10px;">
        <?php if($paginationObj->getFirstPage() !=
                                $paginationObj->getPage()): ?>
        <?php echo link_to('&laquo;',
                    '@menu?page='.$paginationObj->getFirstPage(),
                    'class="pageLink"') ?>
        <?php echo link_to('&lt;',
                    '@menu?page='.$paginationObj->getPreviousPage(),
                    'class="pageLink"') ?>
        <?php endif ?>

        <?php $links = $paginationObj->getLinks();
            foreach ($links as $page): ?>
        <?php echo ($page == $paginationObj->getPage()) ?
            '<span class="selectedPageBox">'.$page.'</span>' :
            link_to($page, '@menu?page='.$page ,
                    'class="pageLink"')?>
        <?php endforeach ?>

        <?php if($paginationObj->getLastPage() !=
                                $paginationObj->getPage()): ?>
            <?php echo link_to('&gt;',
                    '@menu?page='.$paginationObj->getNextPage(),
                    'class="pageLink"') ?>
            <?php echo link_to('&raquo;',
                    '@menu?page='.$paginationObj->getLastPage(),
                    'class="pageLink"') ?>
        <?php endif ?>
    </div>
<?php endif ?>
```

The Propel pager object has everything we need for our template. So let's quickly run over them:

Propel pager object functions	Description
`$paginationObj->haveToPaginate()`	This function returns a Boolean that tests whether or not there are pages to paginate
`$paginationObj->getFirstPage()`	The first page number for use is 1
`$paginationObj->getNextPage()`	When looping will provide the next page to where the user is on
`$paginationObj->getPreviousPage()`	When looping will provide the previous page to where the user is on
`$paginationObj->getPage()`	This function gets the current page that the user is on
`$paginationObj->getLastPage()`	This function gets the last page
`$paginationObj->getNbResults()`	Total amount of pages

As we now need to pass in the page parameter as a part of the URL, we do so by partly creating an old-style URL.

Look at the `link_to()` helper to see how we will now reference a routing rule that requires a parameter. The helper essentially takes an old-formatted URL string and turns it into a friendly URL.

```php
<?php echo link_to('&gt;',
                   '@menu?page='.$paginationObj->getNextPage(),
                   'class="pageLink"') ?>
```

Symfony will turn this code into /menu/1 rather than /menu?page=1.

By using the methods above and a little logic, we have created pagination on our menu page.

Before viewing the page, let's add some CSS. Open the default `main.css` file located in `web/css/` and add the following CSS:

```css
.selectedPageBox{
        padding: 3px 6px;
        border: 1px solid #000000;
        background-color: #000000;
        color: #ffffff;
        }


        a.pageLink:link{
                padding: 3px 6px;
                border: 1px solid #000000;
```

```
            background-color: #ffffff;
            color: #000000;
            text-decoration: none;
    }

    a.pageLink:visited{
            padding: 3px 6px;
            border: 1px solid #000000;
            background-color: #ffffff;
            color: #000000;
            text-decoration: none;

    }

    a.pageLink:hover{
            padding: 3px 6px;
            border: 1px solid #000000;
            background-color: #000000;
            color: #ffffff;
            text-decoration: none;

    }
```

Now let's take a look at the finished template in `indexSuccess.php`:

```php
<?php $i=0 ?>

<?php foreach($milkshakeObj->getResults() as $milkshake): ?>
    <div style="width: 176px; float: left; padding-bottom: 20px;
        margin-right: 16px; margin-bottom: 16px;">
      <div style="height: 250px; ">
         <?php echo image_tag('/images/'.$milkshake->getImageUrl(),
                        array('alt'=>$milkshake->getName())); ?>
      </div>
      <div>
        Name:<?php echo link_to($milkshake->getName(),
                        'menu_item', $milkshake) ?><br />
        Calories: <?php echo $milkshake->getCalories() ?>
      </div>
    </div>

    <?php if(($i%3) == 2): ?>
        <div style="clear:both"></div>
    <?php endif ?>

  <?php $i++ ?>

<?php endforeach; ?>

<?php include_partial('global/pagination',
                    array('paginationObj'=>$milkshakeObj)) ?>
```

With everything in place, browse to `http://milkshake/frontend_dev.php/menu` or click on the **Menu** link. You should see the following:

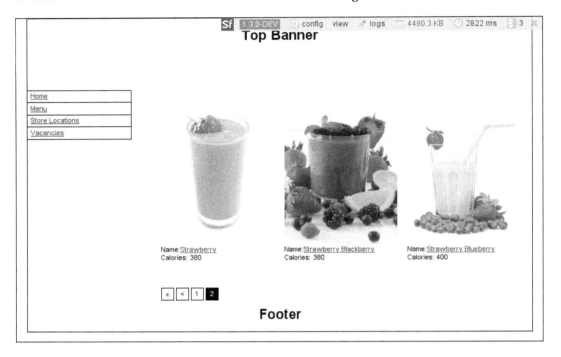

Creating the milkshake page

We need a nice, user-friendly URL that will enable the user to browse to the page for a selected milkshake. One bad practice is to have the ID in the URL. So to construct the URL for each milkshake page, we are going to use a slug. Essentially, a **slug** is a URL-friendly string and we are going to base it on the milkshake name. There are a few ways to achieve this. We are going to tackle it by creating another column in the milkshake table named `url_slug` to store the value. Adding this new column is very straightforward. We simply add the column to the schema and then rebuild the models. After that, we build the tables before inserting the data in the fixtures file.

However, introducing the slug will require a few additional changes. As the DAO calls the setter method for the `slug_url` column, we would also like it to transform the `slug_url` into its URL-friendly counterpart by removing any non-alphanumeric characters.

As we are modifying the table, I am also going to insert another column to act as a counter. This will let us know which milkshake has the most views.

Open up the `schema.xml` file in the `config/` folder and add the following columns to the milkshakes table:

```
<column name="url_slug" type="VARCHAR" size="100" required="true" />
<column name="views" type="INTEGER" default="0"/>
```

Next, rebuild the models, forms, filters, and SQL using this:

```
$/home/timmy/workspace/milkshake>symfony propel:build-all-load --no-
confirmation
```

The base milkshake models are now updated. To test this, we will have to insert more data into the `fixtures.yml` file and then amend the DAO. Open the `fixtures.yml` file in the `data/fixture` folder and add a `url_slug` attribute and value for each milkshake. Here is what I added:

```
MilkShake:
  m1:
    name: Blueberry
    url_slug: sfdgsdg @2342sdfaT44444TTasdfsf & adsfasfasfd'' asdfasf
    calories: 200
    image_url: blueberry.jpg
  m2:
    name: Chocolate Digestive
    url_slug: Chocolate Flavor
    calories: 400
    image_url: chocolate_digestive.jpg
  m3:
    name: Raspberry
    url_slug: raspberry flavor
    calories: 250
        image_url: raspberry.jpg
```

I know what you're thinking: There is a blatant error with the `url_slug` attribute on the first milkshake. The reason I have added a string containing alphanumeric and special characters is because the person administrating this could potentially add a special character. (Of course, no one relies on JavaScript, right?) Also, this entry will test our function too.

Before we can get Symfony to insert our data, we must override the `setUrlSlug()` function to convert our string. Therefore, open up the custom DAO `MilkShake.php` in the `lib/model/` folder and add the following:

```
public function setUrlSlug($v)
  {
    //Remove all non-alphanumeric characters except for a space.

    $newV = preg_replace('/\s+/', '-', $v);
    $newV = preg_replace('/[^a-zA-Z0-9\-]/', '', $newV);

    // trim and lowercase
    $newV = strtolower(trim($newV, '-'));

    return parent::setUrlSlug($newV);
  }
```

Our `setUrlSlug()` function overrides the parent function to transform the string for us before passing it back to the parent function.

We are now ready to populate the table with the new fixtures. This time we cannot just load the data, as a referential integrity error will be called. Therefore, let's rebuild the tables and then insert the data:

$/home/timmy/workspace/milkshake>symfony propel:insert-sql --no-confirmation

$/home/timmy/workspace/milkshake>symfony propel:data-load

Routing with an object

We have already seen how to add a routing rule with a variable in the URL pattern when we added pagination. If we had a much larger model and our URL pattern consisted of four or five variables, the template string would have started to bloat. Therefore, we are going to use `sfPropelRoute` rather than `sfRequestRoute`, as the former represents a Propel object and so is optimized.

Add the following rule for the `menu_item` page underneath the `menu` rule:

```
menu_item:
  url: /menu/milkshake/:url_slug
  class:    sfPropelRoute
   options: { model: MilkShake, type: object }
    param: { module: menu, action: milkshake}
```

 Remember that in the YML files, the tab character is invalid. You must use spaces instead.

There are only three differences to note with this rule:

- The variable name is in the URL pattern. As we are using sfPropelRoute, our route will be based on the milkshake model. Therefore, all the variables in the URL need to reflect the column names in the model.

- We are using the sfPropelRoute classes instead of sfRequestRoute.

- We have included an options array containing the model that the Propel routing is based on. Like all routes, we also have to include the param key so that we can map the URL to the module and action. Our new rule will route the request for the milkshake page to the menu module and execute the milkshake action.

Adding the route to the template

To see this in action, we need to reflect it in the template. On the indexSuccess.php template in the frontend/apps/modules/menu/templates folder, change the following:

```
<?php echo $milkshakeArray->getName() ?>
```

to:

```
<?php echo link_to($milkshake->getName(), 'menu_item', $milkshake) ?>
```

Here I have used the link_to helper, which creates the HTML link for us, just like we did previously. However, this time we reference the route label without the @symbol. Instead, we pass in the object. The sfPropelRoute knows which object to use and bases the variables on the objects' getter methods.

Retrieving many-to-many results

The ORM layer allows us to easily retrieve results from multiple tables that have many-to-many relationships. Our milkshake page will display the milkshake along with all of its associated flavors. Using Propel the traditional way means to place the business login inside the linking object, which in our case is MilkshakeFlavorPeer, and using the doSelectJoinAll() method to query the database. Open the MilkshakeFlavorPeer.php file and create the following function:

```
public static function getMilkshakeFlavor($slug)
{

  $c = new Criteria;
  $c->add(MilkShakePeer::URL_SLUG, $slug);

  return self::doSelectJoinAll($c);
  }
```

As the results are based on the `url_slug`, we need to initialize the `Criteria` object. The `Criteria` has an `add()` method, which represents the `where` clause. The `add()` method would be translated to SQL like this:

```
where url_slug = '$slug'
```

Rather than using the `doSelect()` method, I have used the `doSelectJoinAll()` method, which performs all the necessary joins. There are other similar methods available which you can use depending on your criteria:

- `doSelectJoinMilkshake()`
- `doSelectJoinFlavor()`
- `doSelectJoinAllExceptFlavor()`
- `doSelectJoinAllExceptMilkshake()`

This is all that is required for querying. But we will see the real power in the action and template.

Accessing related objects in the action

With all this in place, the last thing to do is create the action. The last action we created retrieved a result set and passed that to the template. Because we have a views column, the action needs to not only get the milkshake from the table, but also to update the object and save it back to the database. So let's create the milkshake method in our `action.class.php` file:

```php
public function executeMilkshake(sfWebRequest $request)
{
  $this->flavorArray = MilkshakeFlavorPeer::getMilkshakeFlavor(
                       $request->getParameter('url_slug'));

  //Forward to a 404
  $this->forward404If(count($this->flavorArray) < 1);

  //strip from array
  $this->milkshakeObj = $this->flavorArray[0];

  //Set the page title
  $this->getResponse()->setTitle(
     $this->milkshakeObj->getMilkShake()->getName().' Milkshake');

  //Increment the total views
  $total = $this->milkshakeObj->getMilkShake()->getViews() + 1 ;

  //Update the object and save
  $this->milkshakeObj->getMilkShake()->setViews($total);
     $this->milkshakeObj->getMilkShake()->save();

  return sfView::SUCCESS;
}
```

The results in the returned array to `$this->flavorArray` are of the type `MilkshakeFlavor`. We will need to access the related milkshake object and its `Flavor` objects at some point. Propel also provides access methods to retrieve the associated objects in an extremely efficient manner, as we are about to see. Let's look at the code in the action that we have just created:

- `$this->getResponse()->setTitle($this->milkshakeObj->getMilkShake()->getName().' Milkshake');`

  As the title of each milkshake page is going to be dynamic, we will need to set this through the `sfResponse()` object. The method to do this is `setTitle()`. What I have passed into this is the name of the milkshake. To access the title we can use the `getMilkshake()` accessor method, which retrieves the associated milkshake. This *chaining* makes accessing related objects easy.

- `$this->milkshakeObj->getMilkShake()->setViews($total);`

  Setting a value for an object is just as easy as retrieving. Rather than using the getter method, you can call the setter method to set the total views as I have done. At this point, all the total views are set only in the object.

- `$this->milkshakeObj->getMilkShake()->save();`

  To save the modified object back to the database, we use the object's `save()` function. This will now save the object to the database with the incremented view total.

Accessing related objects in the templates

We have made the `MilkshakeFlavor` result object available to the template. So next, we can create the `milkshakeSuccess.php` template in the `apps/frontend/modules/menu/templates/` folder. We'll add the following template code:

```
<div>
  <div style="width: 192px; float: left;">
  <?php echo image_tag('/images/'.$milkshakeObj->getMilkShake()-
>getImageUrl()); ?>
  </div>
  <div style="width: 300px; margin-left: 192px;">
  <h3 style="padding-top:0; margin-top:0">
      <?php echo $milkshakeObj->getMilkShake()->getName() ?></h3>
  Total Calories: <?php echo $milkshakeObj->getMilkShake()->
                              getCalories() ?><br /><br />
  All milkshakes are made with Cornish cream ice cream and full fat
milk. This milkshake also contains:<br />
  <br />
```

```php
<?php foreach($flavorArray as $flavor): ?>
  <strong><?php echo($flavor->getFlavor()->
                          getName()) ?></strong><br />
<?php endforeach ?>

  </div>
  <div style="clear: both"></div>
</div>
```

The first two calls are done through chaining to retrieve the milkshake's name and calorie count. The final part on the template is the retrieval of the flavors. I have looped over the entire result set and used the `getFlavor()` method to access each of the related flavors. Then using the flavor object's getter method `getName()`, we can easily retrieve the name and the related flavor, and echo them out. This will leave us with the following page:

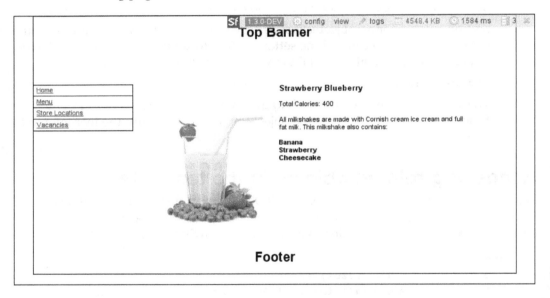

Plugins

One of Symfony's bestselling points is its plugin architecture, not to mention the amount of plugins that are available from the community. There are two types of plugins. One is derived from a module or application, and then packaged up as a fully functional entity. The other type of plugin can be a useful tool to aid in development. Using a plugin could not be simpler. You can either install it via the CLI or download and copy it to the `plugins/` folder, and then enable the plugin in the `settings.yml` file. Rebuild your models and clear the cache, and you're done.

To demonstrate installing and using a plugin, we are going to install `DbFinderPlugin`. `DbFinderPlugin` will be very useful to developers new to Symfony. As mentioned already, there are two ORMs with Doctrine installed by default. By using `DbFinderPlugin`, it will not matter which ORM you choose to start your project in, as the plugin allows you to change it. It also uses a jQuery style syntax and makes caching really easy.

DbFinderPlugin

To install a plugin, you can use the `plugin:install` task:

```
$/home/timmy/workspace/milkshake>symfony plugin:install DbFinderPlugin

$/home/timmy/workspace/milkshake>symfony cc
```

At the time of writing, the `DbFinder` plugin was unavailable to download via the Symfony task. Therefore, I downloaded the plugin from the site and unzipped it into the plugin folder. The plugin can be found at `http://www.symfony-project.org/plugins/DbFinderPlugin`. The folder path after unzipping the plugin is `plugins/DbFinderPlugin/`.

As the first command starts executing, you will see the following in the terminal window:

```
timmy@timmys-laptop:~/workspace/poo$ symfony plugin:install --release="1.2.2" DbFinderPlugin
>> plugin     installing plugin "DbFinderPlugin"
>> sfPearFrontendPlugin Attempting to discover channel "pear.symfony-project.com"...
>> sfPearFrontendPlugin downloading channel.xml ...
>> sfPearFrontendPlugin Starting to download channel.xml (663 bytes)
>> sfPearFrontendPlugin .
>> sfPearFrontendPlugin ...done: 663 bytes
>> sfPearFrontendPlugin Auto-discovered channel "pear.symfony-project.com", alias
>> sfPearFrontendPlugin "symfony", adding to registry
>> sfPearFrontendPlugin Attempting to discover channel
>> sfPearFrontendPlugin "plugins.symfony-project.org"...
>> sfPearFrontendPlugin downloading channel.xml ...
>> sfPearFrontendPlugin Starting to download channel.xml (639 bytes)
>> sfPearFrontendPlugin ...done: 639 bytes
>> sfPearFrontendPlugin Auto-discovered channel "plugins.symfony-project.org", alias
>> sfPearFrontendPlugin "symfony-plugins", adding to registry
>> sfPearFrontendPlugin downloading DbFinderPlugin-1.2.2.tgz ...
>> sfPearFrontendPlugin Starting to download DbFinderPlugin-1.2.2.tgz (74,088 bytes)
>> sfPearFrontendPlugin ...done: 74,088 bytes
>> sfSymfonyPluginManager Installation successful for plugin "DbFinderPlugin"
```

The task downloads and unzips the plugin into the `plugin/pluginname` folder. I will not go into too much detail on how to use the plugin, as there is some very good documentation available on the plugins' community site at `http://www.symfony-project.org/plugins/DbFinderPlugin`.

In the previous chapter, we looked at the project configuration file in `config/ProjectConfiguration.class.php` and noted that the Propel plugin was enabled here. For any plugin to work, it must be listed here. Therefore, let's open the file and add the `DbFinder` plugins as follows:

```
public function setup()
{
    $this->enablePlugins(array('sfPropelPlugin','DbFinderPlugin'));
}
```

Note that because I have added the `DbFinderPlugin` to the list, I have passed in both plugins as an array.

 If you don't pass in the plugins as an array, then they will not be registered.

I have refactored our two custom models. To give you a taste of just how good this plugin is, let's refactor our two functions inside the custom models. Let's start with the `getAllShakes()` method in the `lib/model/MilkShakePeer.php` file and change the present code:

```
//Create the criteria
$c = new Criteria();

//Order by name in ascending order
$c->addAscendingOrderByColumn(self::NAME);

//Create the pager
$pagerObj = new sfPropelPager('MilkShake', $totalItems);
$pagerObj->setCriteria($c);
$pagerObj->setPage($currentPage);
$pagerObj->init();
    return $pagerObj;
```

to:

```
$pagerObj = DbFinder::from('Milkshake')->paginate($currentPage,
                                                  $totalItems);

    return $pagerObj;
```

As you can see, the plugin has enabled us to convert 13 lines down into 3 lines. Also, the jQuery-style chaining syntax makes your code very easy to read. The other model where we added custom business logic is the `getMilkshakeFlavor()` method in the `MilkshakeFlavorPeer.php` file. Let's change the code from:

```
$c = new Criteria;
    $c->add(MilkShakePeer::URL_SLUG, $slug);

    return self::doSelectJoinAll($c);
```

to:

```
return DbFinder::from('MilkshakeFlavor')->with('Milkshake')-
>with('Flavor')->where('Milkshake.UrlSlug', $slug)->find();
```

If the line is too long, you could format it slightly like this:

```
return DbFinder::from('MilkshakeFlavor')
    ->with('Milkshake')
    ->with('Flavor')
    ->where('Milkshake.UrlSlug', $slug)
    ->find();
```

Again, you can see that the plugin has allowed us to condense our code, even while making the code readable. (Not that it was not really needed here, but has made the code uniform.)

Finishing off the location page

Another page that needs to be finished is the location's page. Once again, we start with the model, add the action, and then create the template.

Let's open `lib/model/StoreLocationPeer.php` and create a custom method called `getAllLocations()` that will retrieve all locations, and order them by country and city. Again, we will be using `DbFinder` to handle this for us.

```
    /*
     * Get all locations
     *
     * @return Array Array of result objects.
     */
    public static function getAllLocations()
    {
        $locations = DbFinder::from('StoreLocation')->
                            orderBy('Country')->
                            orderBy('City')->find();
        return    $locations;
    }
```

The methods of DbFinder should be clear. We are querying the store_locations table, which is represented by the StoreLocation model. We then order by Country and City. Next, we need to create the action in apps/frontend/modules/location/actions/actions.class.php. As we are going to use the index action, we can add the application logic inside this action.

```php
public function executeIndex(sfWebRequest $request)
{
    $this->locationsArray = StoreLocationPeer::getAllLocations();

    return sfView::SUCCESS;
}
```

I have only added the logic to call our StoreLocation model. We now need to add the template logic to the actions template in apps/frontend/modules/location/templates/indexSuccess.php. Here we need to loop over the results that have been returned, just like we did on the menu page.

```php
<h3 style="margin-top:0; padding-top:0">We are currently in</h3>

<?php foreach ($locationsArray as $location): ?>
<div style="margin-bottom: 16px;">
    <?php echo $location->getAddress1(); ?><br />
    <?php echo ($location->getAddress2() != "")?
                $location->getAddress2(). "<br />": ""; ?>
    <?php echo ($location->getAddress3() != "")?
                $location->getAddress3(). "<br />": ""; ?>
    <?php echo $location->getCity(); ?><br />
    <?php echo $location->getPostcode(); ?><br />
    <?php echo $location->getCountry(); ?><br />
    <?php echo $location->getPhone(); ?><br />
    <?php echo $location->getFax(); ?><br />
</div>
<?php endforeach ?>
```

We have used a simple foreach() loop in the template to loop over the result set and the getter methods to retrieve the values. I have also included the logic that will prevent a blank line from being displayed if the Address2 or Address3 columns contain no data. Now back to the browser, let's click on the **Store Locations** link in the navigation. Here you will see all the locations ordered by country and then city.

Summary

We have seen how quickly and easily we can get a dynamic web site up and running with Symfony. We have addressed populating your database with test data and building all of the ORM models. Using these models, we have created our business logic for accessing the database.

It was simple not only to retrieve basic results, but also many-to-many results. We have also seen how the `Criteria` object is used to generate a query and the hydration process that sits behind everything.

The application logic was also very straightforward. As you will probably agree, the separation of code means different developers will not stray too far.

We ended by demonstrating an extension to Symfony — plugins. We installed the `DbFinder` plugin to show you a well-used plugin, and how to install and configure it.

4
User Interaction and Email Automation

Up until now, we have covered the basics for you to get a dynamic web site up and running. One thing that we have not looked at yet is the creation of forms. Symfony incorporates a subframework that handles forms, which once mastered, makes creating forms an enjoyable task. In this chapter we are going to see how easy it is to create and validate forms by creating a newsletter signup module for our web site. In the previous chapter we looked at plugins and learnt how useful they can be. Therefore, we will then convert our new module into a plugin so that we can use it with other projects.

By the end of this chapter you will know how to:

- Add a third-party library to send automated emails
- Create and modify Propel-based forms
- Use flash variables
- Create a plugin and package it up for redistribution

The signup module

We want to provide the users with the functionality to enter their name, email address, and how they found our web site. We want all this stored in a database and to have an email automatically sent out to the users thanking them for signing up..

To start things off, we must first add some new tables to our existing database schema.

The structure of our newsletter table will be straightforward. We will need one table to capture the users' information and a related table that will hold the names of all the places where we advertised our site. I have constructed the following entity relationship diagram to show you a visual relationship of the tables:

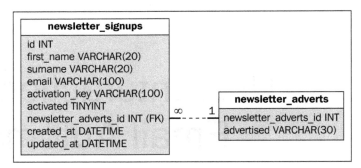

Let's translate this diagram into XML and place it in the `config/schema.xml` file:

```
<table name="newsletter_adverts" idMethod="native"
        phpName="NewsletterAds">
    <column name="newsletter_adverts_id" type="INTEGER"
            required="true" autoIncrement="true"
            primaryKey="true" />
    <column name="advertised" type="VARCHAR" size="30"
            required="true" />
</table>

<table name="newsletter_signups" idMethod="native"
        phpName="NewsletterSignup">
    <column name="id" type="INTEGER" required="true"
            autoIncrement="true" primaryKey="true" />
    <column name="first_name" type="VARCHAR" size="20"
            required="true" />
    <column name="surname" type="VARCHAR" size="20"
            required="true" />
    <column name="email" type="VARCHAR" size="100"
            required="true" />
    <column name="activation_key" type="VARCHAR" size="100"
            required="true" />
    <column name="activated" type="BOOLEAN" default="0"
            required="true" />

    <column name="newsletter_adverts_id" type="INTEGER"
            required="true"/>
```

```
<foreign-key foreignTable="newsletter_adverts"
             onDelete="CASCADE">
  <reference local="newsletter_adverts_id"
             foreign="newsletter_adverts_id" />
</foreign-key>
<column name="created_at" type="TIMESTAMP" required="true" />
<column name="updated_at" type="TIMESTAMP" required="true" />
</table>
```

We will need to populate the `newsletter_adverts` table with some test data as well. Therefore, I have also appended the following data to the `fixtures.yml` file located in the `data/fixtures/` directory:

```
NewsletterAds:
  nsa1:
    advertised: Internet Search
  nsa2:
    advertised: High Street
  nsa3:
    advertised: Poster
```

With the database schema and the test data ready to be inserted into the database, we can once again use the Symfony tasks. As we have added two new tables to the schema, we will have to rebuild everything to generate the models using the following command:

```
$/home/timmy/workspace/milkshake>symfony propel:build-all-load --no-
confirmation
```

Now we have populated the tables in the database, and the models and forms have been generated for use too.

Binding a form to a database table

Symfony contains a whole framework just for the development of forms. The forms framework makes building forms easier by applying object-oriented methods to their development. Each form class is based on its related table in the database. This includes the fields, the validators, and the way in which the forms and fields are rendered.

A look at the generated base class

Rather than starting off with a simple form, we are going to look at the base form class that has already been generated for us as a part of the build task we executed earlier. Because the code is generated, it will be easier for you to see the initial flow of a form. So let's open the base class for the `NewsletterSignupForm` form. The file is located at `lib/form/base/BaseNewsletterSignupForm.class.php`:

```php
class BaseNewsletterSignupForm extends BaseFormPropel
{
  public function setup()
  {
    $this->setWidgets(array(
      'id'                   => new sfWidgetFormInputHidden(),
      'first_name'           => new sfWidgetFormInput(),
      'surname'              => new sfWidgetFormInput(),
      'email'                => new sfWidgetFormInput(),
      'activation_key'       => new sfWidgetFormInput(),
      'activated'            => new sfWidgetFormInputCheckbox(),
      'newsletter_adverts_id' => new sfWidgetFormPropelChoice
          (array('model' => 'NewsletterAds', 'add_empty' => false)),
      'created_at'           => new sfWidgetFormDateTime(),
      'updated_at'           => new sfWidgetFormDateTime(),
    ));

  $this->setValidators(array(
   'id' => new sfValidatorPropelChoice(array
           ('model' => 'NewsletterSignup', 'column' => 'id',
                                        'required' => false)),
   'first_name' => new sfValidatorString(array('max_length' => 20)),
   'surname'    => new sfValidatorString(array('max_length' => 20)),
   'email'      => new sfValidatorString(array('max_length' => 100)),
   'activation_key' => new sfValidatorString(array('max_length' => 100)),
   'activated'              => new sfValidatorBoolean(),
   'newsletter_adverts_id'=> new sfValidatorPropelChoice(array
                              ('model' => 'NewsletterAds',
                               'column' => 'newsletter_adverts_id')),
    'created_at'           => new sfValidatorDateTime(),
    'updated_at'           => new sfValidatorDateTime(),
  ));

  $this->widgetSchema->setNameFormat('newsletter_signup[%s]');

  $this->errorSchema = new sfValidatorErrorSchema
                          ($this->validatorSchema);

  parent::setup();
  }
```

There are five areas in this base class that are worth noting:

- This base class extends the `BaseFormPropel` class, which is an empty class. All base classes extend this class, which allows us to add global settings to all our forms.

- All of the columns in our table are treated as fields in the form, and are referred to as widgets. All of these widgets are then attached to the form by adding them to the `setWidgets()` method. Looking over the widgets in the array, you will see that they are pretty standard, such as `sfWidgetFormInputHidden()`, `sfWidgetFormInput()`.

- However, there is one widget added that follows the relationship between the `newsletter_sigups` table and the `newsletter_adverts` table. It is the `sfWidgetFormPropelChoice` widget. Because there is a 1:M relation between the tables, the default behavior is to use this widget, which creates an HTML drop-down box and is populated with the values from the `newsletter_adverts` table. As a part of the attribute set, you will see that it has set the model needed to retrieve the values to `NewsletterAds` and the `newsletter_adverts_id` column for the actual values of the drop-down box.

- All the widgets on the form must be validated by default. To do this, we have to call the `setValidators()` method and add the validation requirements to each widget. At the moment, the generated validators reflect the attributes of our database as set in the schema. For example, the `first_name` field in the statement `'first_name' => new sfValidatorString(array('max_length' => 20))` demonstrates that the validator checks if the maximum length is 20. If you remember, in our schema too, the `first_name` column is set to `20` characters.

- The final part calls the parent's `setup()` function.

The base class `BaseNewsletterSignupForm` contains all the components needed to generate the form for us. So let's get the form on a page and take a look at the method to customize it.

 There are many widgets that Symfony provides for us. You can find the classes for them inside the `widget/` directory of your Symfony installation. The Symfony `propel` task always generates a form class and its corresponding base class. Of course, not all of our tables will need to have a form bound to them. Therefore, delete all the form classes that are not needed.

Rendering the form

Rendering this basic form requires us to instantiate the form object in the action. Assigning the form object to the global `$this` variable means that we can pass the form object to the template just like any other variable. So let's start by implementing the newsletter signup module. In your terminal window, execute the `generate:module` task like this:

```
$/home/timmy/workspace/milkshake>symfony generate:module frontend signup
```

Now we can start with the application logic. Open the action class from `apps/frontend/modules/signup/actions/actions.class.php` for the signup module and add the following logic inside the index action:

```
public function executeIndex(sfWebRequest $request)
{
  $this->form = new NewsletterSignupForm();
  return sfView::SUCCESS;
}
```

As I had mentioned earlier, the form class deals with the form validation and rendering. For the time being, we are going to stick to the default layout by allowing the form object to render itself. Using this method initially will allow us to create rapid prototypes. Let's open the `apps/frontend/signup/templates/indexSuccess.php` template and add the following view logic:

```
<form action="<?php echo url_for('signup/submit') ?>" method="POST">
  <table><?php echo $form ?></table>
  <input type="submit" />
</form>
```

The form class is responsible for rendering of the form elements only. Therefore, we have to include the `<form>` and `submit` HTML tags that wrap around the form. Also, the default format of the form is set to 'table'. Again, we must also add the start and end tags of the `<table>`.

At this stage, we would normally be able to view the form in the browser. But doing so will raise a Symfony exception error. The cause of this is that the results retrieved from the `newsletter_adverts` table are in the form of an array of objects. These results need to populate the select box widget. But in the current format, this is not possible. Therefore, we have to convert each object into its string equivalent. To do this, we need to create a PHP magic function of `__toString()` in the DAO class `NewsletterAds`.

The DAO class for NewlsetterAds is located at lib/model/NewsletterAds.php just as all of the other models. Here we need to represent each object as its name, which is the value in the advertised column. Remember that we need to add this method to the DAO class as this represents a row within the results, unlike the peer class that represents the entire result set. Let's add the function to the NewsletterAds class as I have done here:

```
class NewsletterAds extends BaseNewsletterAds
{
  public function __toString()
  {
    return $this->getAdvertised();
  }
}
```

We are now ready to view the completed form. In your web browser, enter the URL http://milkshake/frontend_dev.php/signup and you will see the result shown in the following screenshot:

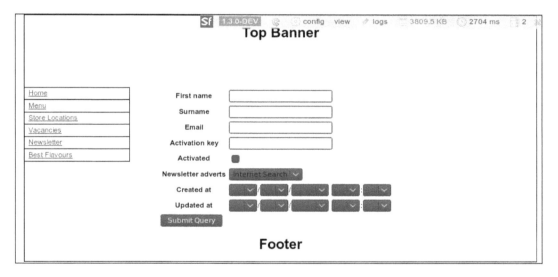

As you can see, although the form has been rendered according to our table structure, the fields which we do not want the user to fill in are also included. Of course, we can change this quiet easily. But before we take a look at the layout of the form, let's customize the widgets and widget validators. Now we can begin working on the application logic for submitting the form.

Customizing form widgets and validators

All of the generated form classes are located in the `lib/form` and the `lib/form/base` directories. The latter is where the default generated classes are located, and the former is where the customizable classes are located. This follows the same structure as the models.

Each custom form class inherits from its parent. Therefore, we have to override some of the functions to customize the form.

Let's customize the widgets and validators for the `NewsletterSignupForm`. Open the `lib/forms/NewsletterSignupForm.class.php` file and paste the following code inside the `configure()` method:

```
//Removed unneeded widgets
  unset(
    $this['created_at'], $this['updated_at'],
    $this['activation_key'], $this['activated'], $this['id']
  );

  //Set widgets

//Modify widgets
  $this->widgetSchema['first_name'] = new sfWidgetFormInput();
  $this->widgetSchema['newsletter_adverts_id'] = new
    sfWidgetFormPropelChoice(array('model' => 'NewsletterAds',
      'add_empty' => true, 'label'=>'Where did you find us?'));
  $this->widgetSchema['email'] = new sfWidgetFormInput
              (array('label' => 'Email Address'));

  //Add validation
  $this->setValidators(array
    ('first_name'=> new sfValidatorString(array
      ('required' => true), array('required' => 'Enter your
                                               firstname')),
    'surname'=> new sfValidatorString(array('required' => true),
                array('required' => 'Enter your surname')),
    'email'=> new sfValidatorString(array('required' => true),
                array('invalid' => 'Provide a valid email',
                      'required' => 'Enter your email')),
    'newsletter_adverts_id' => new
      sfValidatorPropelChoice(array('model' => 'NewsletterAds',
            'column' => 'newsletter_adverts_id'),
            array('required' => 'Select where you found us')),
  ));

  //Set post validators
  $this->validatorSchema->setPostValidator(
```

```
   new sfValidatorPropelUnique(array('model' =>
     'NewsletterSignup', 'column' => array('email')),
      array('invalid' => 'Email address is already registered'))
   );

//Set form name
$this->widgetSchema->setNameFormat('newsletter_signup[%s]');

//Set the form format
$this->widgetSchema->setFormFormatterName('list');
```

Let's take a closer look at the code.

Removing unneeded fields

To remove the fields that we do not want to be rendered, we must call the PHP unset() method and pass in the fields to unset. As mentioned earlier, all of the fields that are rendered need a corresponding validator, unless we unset them. Here we do not want the created_at and activation_key fields to be entered by the user. To do so, the unset() method should contain the following code:

```
unset(
    $this['created_at'], $this['updated_at'],
    $this['activation_key'], $this['activated'], $this['id']
);
```

Modifying the form widgets

Although it'll be fine to use the remaining widgets as they are, let's have a look at how we can modify them:

```
//Modify widgets
    $this->widgetSchema['first_name'] = new sfWidgetFormInput();
    $this->widgetSchema['newsletter_adverts_id'] = new
      sfWidgetFormPropelChoice(array('model' =>
      'AlSignupNewsletterAds', 'add_empty' => true,
      'label'=>'Where did you find us?'));
    $this->widgetSchema['email'] = new
      sfWidgetFormInput(array('label' => 'Email Address'));
```

There are several types of widgets available, but our form requires only two of them. Here we have used the sfWidgetFormInput() and sfWidgetFormPropelChoice() widgets. Each of these can be initialized with several values. We have initialized the email and newsletter_adverts_id widgets with a label. This basically renders the label field associated to the widget on the form. We do not have to include a label because Symfony adds the label according to the column name.

Adding form validators

Let's add the validators in a similar way as we have added the widgets:

```
//Add validation
$this->setValidators(array(
  'first_name'=> new sfValidatorString(array('required' => true),
                   array('required' => 'Enter your firstname')),
  'surname'=> new sfValidatorString(array('required' => true),
                   array('required' => 'Enter your surname')),
  'email'=> new sfValidatorEmail(array('required' => true),
                   array('invalid' => 'Provide a valid email',
                   'required' => 'Enter your email')),
  'newsletter_adverts_id' => new sfValidatorPropelChoice(array
           ('model' => 'NewsletterAds',
               'column' => 'newsletter_adverts_id'),
               array('required' => 'Select where you found us')),
  ));
//Set post validators
$this->validatorSchema->setPostValidator(new
       sfValidatorPropelUnique(array('model' => 'NewsletterSignup',
       'column' => array('email')),
       array('invalid' => 'Email address is already registered'))
   );
```

Our form will need four different types of validators:

- `sfValidatorString`: This checks the validity of a string against a criteria. It takes four arguments—required, trim, min_length, and max_length.
- `SfValidatorEmail`: This validates the input against the pattern of an email address.
- `SfValidatorPropelChoice`: It validates the value with the values in the `newsletter_adverts` table. It needs the model and column that are to be used.
- `SfValidatorPropelUnique`: Again, this validator checks the value against the values in a given table column for uniqueness. In our case, we want to use the `NewsletterSignup` model to test if the email column is unique.

As mentioned earlier, all the fields must have a validator. Although it's not recommended, you can allow extra parameters to be passed in. To achieve this, there are two steps:

1. You must disable the default option of having all fields validated by `$this->validatorSchema->setOption('allow_extra_fields', true)`.
2. Although the above step allows the values to bypass validation, they will be filtered out of the results. To prevent this, you will have to set `$this->validatorSchema->setOption('filter_extra_fields', false)`.

Form naming convention and setting its style

The final part we added is the naming convention for the HTML attributes and the style in which we want the form rendered. The HTML output will use our naming convention. For example, in the following code, we have set the convention to `newsletter_signup[fieldname]` for each input field's name.

```
//Set form name
$this->widgetSchema->setNameFormat('newsletter_signup[%s]');

//Set the form format
$this->widgetSchema->setFormFormatterName('list');
```

Two formats are shipped with Symfony that we can use to render our form. We can either render it in an HTML table or an unordered list. As we have seen, the default is an HTML table. But by setting this as `list`, the form is now rendered as an unordered HTML list, just like the following screenshot. (Of course, I had to replace the `<table>` tags with the `<ul>` tags.)

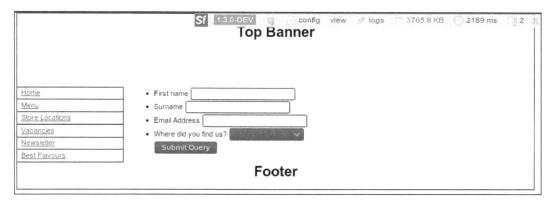

Submitting the form

Now that we have the form rendered on our template, we need to handle the application logic for submitting the form. The first step is to add the routing rules for our form page and its submission. The form sits within the signup module, and therefore, we will keep all of the functionality there too. Open the routing file `apps/frontend/config/routing.yml`, and add the following routes:

```
signup:
  url:  /signup
  param: { module: signup, action: index}

signup_submit:
  url:  /signup/submit
  param: { module: signup, action: submit}
```

Here we have created two rules, `signup` and `signup_submit`. The first rule will be routed to the `index` action and the second will be routed to the `submit` action in our signup module.

Next, we will create the `submit` action. Open up the actions class from `apps/frontend/modules/signup/actions/actions.class.php` and create the `submit` action:

```
public function executeSubmit(sfWebRequest $request)
{
   $this->form = new NewsletterSignupForm();
    if ($request->isMethod('post') && $this->form->bindAndSave
         ($request->getParameter($this->form->getName())))
    {
       $this->redirect('signup@');
    }
    //Use the index template as it contains the form
    $this->setTemplate('index');
}
```

Looking over the application logic of our `submit` action, we first need to instantiate `NewsletterSignupForm`, after which we will do two things. First, we will test the `request` method as the form should be a `post`. This is handled by the `$request->isMethod('post')` method. Secondly, we need to bind the submitted and cleaned form values to the form that we just instantiated. There are two ways to do this:

- The first method is to use the `bind()` function. This will only bind the cleaned values to the form for us. After this, we would need to call the form's `save()` method to save the form to the database.

- The second method, which is a little cleaner (and the one I prefer to use), is the form's `bindAndSave()` method that handles the binding and saving for us.

If the request is a `post` and the form is valid, the `redirect()` method is called. (Notice how we can also add the routing label to this method.) We use this method because it forces a redirect, which means if the user clicks on the refresh button, the form will not be re-submitted.

If you wanted to display a thank you page, you can, of course, create another action and a template to handle this. But we will address this later in the chapter.

You should now be able to go ahead and test the form. In the following screenshot, I have tried to submit the form without a **Surname** and an incomplete **Email Address**, which resulted in the anticipated errors:

Changing the global rendering of forms

So far, we have seen how forms are rendered globally, either as a table or an unordered list. Of course, the forms framework makes the global rendering of forms very easy to change and extend. To demonstrate this, we are going to create our own format. This new format will render the fields within the `<div>` tags.

To create our own form format, we need to create a new class that extends the `sfWidgetFormSchemaFormatter` class. The naming convention for the actual class that we will create needs to follow `sfWidgetFormSchemaFormatter`**Name**. Therefore, our class will be called `sfWidgetFormSchemaFormatter`**Div**`.class.php`. Because this class will need to be accessed globally, it must be placed in either the `lib/` folder or in a subfolder within the `lib/` directory. Create a new folder in the `lib/` directory called `widget`, so that the path reflects `lib/widget`. In this folder, we are going to create our formatter class. Create a file named `WidgetFormSchemaFormatterDiv.class.php` in the newly created `widget/` directory. Open the new file and create the following class:

```php
<?php
class sfWidgetFormSchemaFormatterDiv extends
sfWidgetFormSchemaFormatter
{
protected
    $rowFormat = '<div style="padding-bottom: 10px;
                height: 20px;"><div style="width: 150px;
                float: left;">%label% </div>
            <div style="width: 300px; float: left">
                %field% %error% <br />%help%</div>
```

```
                         <div style="clear: both"></div></div>',
      $helpFormat = '<span class="help">%help%</span>',
      $errorRowFormat = '<div>%errors%</div>',
      $errorListFormatInARow = '%errors%',
      $errorRowFormatInARow = '<span class="errorMessage">*%error%
                             </span>',
      $namedErrorRowFormatInARow = '%name%: %error%',
      $decoratorFormat = '<div id="formContainer">%content%</div>';
    }
?>
```

Each variable holds a part of the form. I have added the row formatting to the `$rowFormat` variable. The other variables hold the error messages for the row and the container.

With our new formatter now available, we just have to update the `NewsletterSignupForm.class.php` file so that it is able to use it. Change the following line

```
$this->widgetSchema->setFormFormatterName('list');
```

to:

```
$this->widgetSchema->setFormFormatterName('div');
```

The final part is to style the error message. In the formatter, I have used a reference to a CSS class called `errorMessage`. Therefore, in the `web/css/main.css` file in our stylesheet, I have added the following code:

```
.errorMessage{ color: red; font-weight: bold}
```

After refreshing your browser on the signup page (`http://milkshake/frontend_dev.php/signup`), you will see the new layout along with the validation errors as shown in the following screenshot:

Customizing the rendering of the form

Till now the rendering of forms has all been handled by the default rendering method. From a prototype point of view, this method has allowed us to create a nice, clean form. The only problem we now face is that there are situations where this rendering is not flexible enough.

To render the form, we have been echoing the $form object in the template. This, in fact, is a shortcut to $form->render(). However, there are several rendering functions available for use. We will be using these to customize our form on the template further. To demonstrate this, I will apply these functions to the email field before presenting to you the final version.

The email section of the form can be broken up into three areas: the label, the form field, and the error message. We are going to use three of the rendering functions to completely customize the email section:

- **Setting a label**: For setting the label, we can use the $form['email']->renderLabel() function. You can also customize the label through this function by changing the label and adding the other HTML attributes; for example, $form['email']->renderLabel('Your first name') or $form['email']->renderLabel(null, array('class'=>'myClass')). Of course, this can be set in the form class itself. If it is not set then Symfony will render its column name. The column in our database for this field is called email, which results in 'Email' being returned. For example, if you had a column named email_address, letting Symfony render it would result in 'Email Address' being returned.

- **Displaying the field**: Each field can be called by using $form['email']->render() or $form['email'] for short. Once again, the attributes can be passed in as parameters.

- **Handling the error messages**: To test if the field does contain an error, we can use the $form['email']->hasError() method. To display the actual error message, we must then call the $form['email']->getError() method.

With this in mind for the moment, I am now going to show you how we will render the email row on our form:

```
<div style="height: 30px;">
<div style="width: 150px; float: left"><?php echo $form['email']->
                                        renderLabel() ?></div>
    <?php echo $form['email']->render(($form['email']->hasError())?
        array('class'=>'boxError'): array('class'=>'box')) ?>
    <?php echo ($form['email']->hasError())?
```

```
    ' <span class="errorMessage">* '.$form['email']->getError().
    '</span>': '' ?>
    </div>
    <div style="clear: both"></div>
</div>
```

As you can see, we now have a complete control over how a form is rendered. To complete rendering, I have applied this technique to the other form fields too with the following code:

```
<form action="<?php echo url_for('@signup_submit') ?>" method="post"
    name="Newsletter">
    <div style="height: 30px;">
        <div style="width: 150px; float: left">
          <?php echo $form['first_name']->renderLabel() ?></div>
        <?php echo $form['first_name']->render(($form['first_name']->
            hasError())? array('class'=>'boxError'):
            array('class'=>'box')) ?>
          <?php echo ($form['first_name']->hasError())?
            ' <span class="errorMessage">* '.$form['first_name']->
                                        getError(). '</span>': '' ?>
        <div style="clear: both"></div>
    </div>
    <div style="height: 30px;">
        <div style="width: 150px; float: left">
          <?php echo $form['surname']->renderLabel() ?></div>
        <div style="width: 300px; float: left;">
          <?php echo $form['surname']->render(($form['surname']->
            hasError())? array('class'=>'boxError'):
            array('class'=>'box')) ?>
          <?php echo ($form['surname']->hasError())?
            ' <span class="errorMessage">*
            '.$form['surname']->getError(). '</span>': '' ?>
        </div>
        <div style="clear: both"></div>
    </div>
    <div style="height: 30px;">
        <div style="width: 150px; float: left">
          <?php echo $form['email']->renderLabel() ?></div>
          <?php echo $form['email']->render(($form['email']->
            hasError())? array('class'=>'boxError'):
            array('class'=>'box')) ?>
          <?php echo ($form['email']->hasError())?
            ' <span class="errorMessage">* '.$form['email']->
            getError(). '</span>': '' ?>
        </div>
        <div style="clear: both"></div>
    </div>
    <div style="height: 30px;">
        <div style="width: 150px; float: left">
```

```
            <?php echo $form['newsletter_adverts_id']->renderLabel() ?>
        </div>
            <?php echo $form['newsletter_adverts_id']->
                render(($form['newsletter_adverts_id']->hasError())?
                array('class'=>'boxError'): array('class'=>'box')) ?>
            <?php echo ($form['newsletter_adverts_id']->hasError())?
            ' <span class="errorMessage">*
            '.$form['newsletter_adverts_id']->getError().
                                        '</span>': '' ?>
        <div style="clear: both"></div>
    </div>
    <?php echo $form['_csrf_token']; ?>
        <input type="submit" />
    </form>
```

You must have noted that I have added a reference to another CSS class, `boxError`. The following code too has been added to the `main.css` stylesheet located in the `web/css/` directory:

```
.boxError{ border: 2px solid red;}
```

Form security for the user

When we created our project, there were many default settings configured for us. One such setting concerns the forms and **Cross Site Request Forgery (CSRF)**. To help prevent this, all forms must contain a hidden field called `csr_token`. As you can see in our previous form, I have included this hidden field just above the `submit` button. This value is derived from `csrf_secret`, located in the application's `settings` file at `apps/frontend/config/settings.yml`. Although it is randomly generated, it is advised that you should change this.

After you have completed the template by adding the above code and the CSS, check out the form at `http://milkshake/frontend_dev.php/signup` in your browser. In the following screenshot, I have again tried to submit the form containing errors:

As you can see, the error messages appear with a red border around the input fields.

To finish off the signup section, we will need to create a link to the signup page. I have placed my navigation link on the lefthand side of the page along with all the other links. To do this, open up the application layout template from `apps/frontend/templates/layout.php` and add the following underneath the other navigation links:

```
<li style="margin:0;padding:0.25em 0.5em 0.25em 0.5em; width: 150px;
    border-bottom: 1px solid #000000; border-right: 1px
    solid #000000;  ">
  <?php echo link_to('Newsletter', '@signup') ?></li>
```

Notice how we can still use the routing tag name `@signup` to reference the route.

Creating a simple form

We have seen how powerful forms in Symfony are, especially when bounded to a database table. Not all forms, though, will need to reference a database table. Instead, we can create a simple form for which the process is practically the same. The only difference is that we have to manually create the form class.

Just to give you an example, let's say we want to create a simple feedback form that contains three fields called name, email, and message. You would create the new form class at the same place where all of the other form classes are stored — in `lib/form/` — and perhaps, name the file as `FeedbackForm.class.php`. With this created, let's create the class as follows:

```
class FeedbackForm extends BaseForm
{
  public function configure()
  {
    $this->setWidgets(array(
      'name'    => new sfWidgetFormInput(),
      'email'   => new sfWidgetFormInput(),
      'message' => new sfWidgetFormTextarea(),
    ));
    //Add validation
    $this->setValidators(array(
      'name'=> new sfValidatorString(array('required' => true),
               array('required' => 'Enter your firstname')),
      'email'=> new sfValidatorEmail(array
               ('required' => true),
               array('invalid' => 'Provide a valid email',
```

```
                'required' => 'Enter your email')),
    'message'=> new sfValidatorString(array('required' => true),
            array('required' => 'Enter your surname')),
    ));
  $this->widgetSchema->setNameFormat('feedback[%s]');
  //Set the form format
  $this->widgetSchema->setFormFormatterName('div');
  }
}
```

Comparing this to our Propel, the only difference is that the parent class is BaseForm, as the same logic applies to the forms. If you look at the Propel forms class hierarchy too, both eventually extend sfForm, as sfForm is the parent class for all forms.

The form submission process is also handled in exactly the same way as Propel. However, you only need to call the bind() method, as there is no database table to save the form object. The following code shows the form submission process:

```
$this->form = new FeedbackForm();
if($request->isMethod('post') && $this->form->bind
     ($request->getParameter($this->form->getName())))
{

//Code
}
```

There are two possible ways to retrieve the values from a simple form:

- Using the $request object, you can retrieve all of the fields. For example, suppose you wanted to retrieve the email field, you would call $request->getParameter('feedback[email]'). If you wanted to access all of the fields as an array, you would use $request->getParameter('feedback').

- After calling the bind() method, all of the form values are then bound to the form object. To retrieve the email field, for example, you would use $this->form->getValue('email'). For accessing all the values as an array, you would call $this->form->getValues().

Although I have presented you with two ways to retrieve the form values, it is extremely important that you access the form values through the form object as shown in the latter of the two ways. This is because the values there have been cleaned.

Automated email responses

Symfony comes with a default mailer library that is based on Swift Mailer 4, the detailed documentation is available from their web site at `http://swiftmailer.org`.

After a user has signed up to our mailing list, we would like an email verification to be sent to the user's email address. This will inform the user that he/she has signed up, and will also ask him or her to activate their subscription.

To use the library, we have to complete the following three steps:

1. Store the mailing settings in the application settings file.
2. Add the application logic to the action.
3. Create the email template.

Adding the mailer settings to the application

Just like all the previous settings, we should add all the settings for sending emails to the `module.yml` file for the signup module. This will make it easier to implement any modifications required later. Initially, we should set variables like the email subject, the from name, the from address, and whether we want to send out emails within the `dev` environment. I have added the following items to our signup module's setting file, `apps/frontend/config/module.yml`:

```
dev:
  mailer_deliver: true
all:

    mailer_deliver: true
    mailer_subject: Milkshake Newsletter
    mailer_from_name: Tim
    mailer_from_email: no-reply@milkshake
```

All of the settings can be contained under the `all` label. However, you can see that I have introduced a new label called `dev`. These labels represent the environments, and we have just added a specific variable to the `dev` environment. This setting will allow us to eventually turn off the sending of emails while in the `dev` environment.

Creating the application logic

Triggering the email should occur after the user's details have been saved to the database. To demonstrate this, I have added the highlighted amends to the `submit` action in the `apps/frontend/modules/signup/actions/actions.class.php` file, as shown in the following code:

```
public function executeSubmit(sfWebRequest $request)
  {
    $this->form = new NewsletterSignupForm();

    if ($request->isMethod('post') && $this->form->
        bindAndSave($request->getParameter($this->form->
                                        getName()))))
    {

     //Include the swift lib
     require_once('lib/vendor/swift-mailer/lib/swift_init.php');

      try{
       //Sendmail
       $transport = Swift_SendmailTransport::newInstance();
       $mailBody = $this->getPartial('activationEmail',
           array('name' => $this->form->getValue('first_name')));
      $mailer = Swift_Mailer::newInstance($transport);
      $message = Swift_Message::newInstance();
      $message->setSubject(sfConfig::get('app_mailer_subject'));
      $message->setFrom(array(sfConfig::get('app_mailer_from_email')
                        => sfConfig::get('app_mailer_from_name')));
       $message->setTo(array($this->form->getValue('email')=> $this->
                           form->getValue('first_name')));
       $message->setBody($mailBody, 'text/html');

       if(sfConfig::get('app_mailer_deliver'))
               {
         $result = $mailer->send($message);
               }
      }
      catch(Exception $e)
      {
         var_dump($e);
         exit;
      }
    $this->redirect('@signup');
   }
  //Use the index template as it contains the form
  $this->setTemplate('index');
  }
```

Symfony comes with a `sfMailer` class that extends `Swift_Mailer`. To send mails you could simply implement the following Symfony method:

```
$this->getMailer()->composeAndSend('from@example.com',
'to@example.com', 'Subject', 'Body');
```

Let's walk through the process:

1. Instantiate the Swift Mailer.

2. Retrieve the email template (which we will create next) using the `$this->getPartial('activationEmail', array('name' => $this->form->getValue('first_name')))` method. Breaking this down, the function itself retrieves a partial template. The first argument is the name of the template to retrieve (that is `activationEmail` in our example) which, if you remember, means that the template will be called `_activationEmail.php`. The next argument is an array that contains variables related to the partial template. Here, I have set a name variable. The value for the name is important. Notice how I have used the value within the form object to retrieve the `first_name` value. This is because we know that these values have been cleaned and are safe to use.

3. Set the subject, from, to, and the body items. These functions are Swift Mailer specific:

   ° `setSubject()`: It takes a string as an argument for the subject

   ° `setFrom()`: It takes the name and the mailing address

   ° `setTo()`: It takes the name and the mailing address

   ° `setBody()`: It takes the email body and mime type. Here we passed in our template and set the email to text/html

4. Finally we send the email.

 There are more methods in Swift Mailer. Check out the documentation on the Swift Mailer web site (`http://swiftmailer.org/`).

The partial email template

Lastly, we need to create a partial template that will be used in the email body. In the `templates` folder of the signup module, create a file called `_activationEmail.php` and add the following code to it:

```
Hi <?php echo $name; ?>, <br /><br />
Thank you for signing up to our newsletter.

<br /><br />
Thank you,
<br />
<strong>The Team</strong>
```

The partial is no different from a regular template. We could have opted to pass on the body as a string, but using the template keeps our code uniform. Our signup process now incorporates the functionality to send an email.

 The purpose of this example is to show you how to send an automated email using a third-party library. For a real application, you should most certainly implement a two-phase option wherein the user must verify his or her action.

Flashing temporary values

Sometimes it is necessary to set a temporary variable for one request, or make a variable available to another action after forwarding but before having to delete the variable. Symfony provides this level of functionality within the sfUser object known as a flash variable. Once a flash variable has been set, it lasts until the end of the overall request before it is automatically destroyed.

Setting and getting a flash attribute is managed through two of the sfUser methods. Also, you can test for a flash variable's existence using the third method of the methods listed here:

- `$this->getUser()->setFlash($name, $value, $persist = true)`
- `$this->getUser()->getFlash($name)`
- `$this->getUser()->hasFlash($name)`

Although a flash variable will be available by default when a request is forwarded to another action, setting the argument to false will delete the flash variable before it is forwarded.

To demonstrate how useful flash variables can be, let's readdress the signup form. After a user submits the signup form, the form is redisplayed. I further mentioned that you could create another action to handle a 'thank you' template. However, by using a flash variable we will not have to do so.

As a part of the application logic for the form submission, we can set a flash variable. Then after the action redirects the request, the template can test whether there is a flash variable set. If there is one, the template should show a message rather than the form.

Let's add the `$this->getUser()->setFlash()` function to the `submit` action in the `apps/frontend/modules/signup/actions/actions.class.php` file:

```
//Include the swift lib
require_once('lib/vendor/swift-mailer/lib/swift_init.php');
//set Flash
$this->getUser()->setFlash('Form', 'completed');
try{
```

I have added the flash variable just under the `require_once()` statement. After the user has submitted a valid form, this flash variable will be set with the name of the `Form` and have a value `completed`.

Next, we need to address the template logic. The template needs to check whether a flash variable called `Form` is set. If it is not set, the template shows the form. Otherwise it shows a thank you message. This is implemented using the following code:

```
<?php if(!$sf_user->hasFlash('Form')): ?>
<form action="<?php echo url_for('@signup_submit') ?>"
      method="post" name="Newsletter">
   <div style="height: 30px;">
      <div style="width: 150px; float: left">
         <?php echo $form['first_name']->renderLabel() ?></div>
      <?php echo $form['first_name']->render(($form['first_name']->
         hasError())? array('class'=>'boxError'): array
                                              ('class'=>'box')) ?>
         <?php echo ($form['first_name']->hasError())?
         ' <span class="errorMessage">*
         '.$form['first_name']->getError(). '</span>': '' ?>
      <div style="clear: both"></div>
   </div>

. . . .
</form>
<?php else: ?>
<h1>Thank you</h1>
You are now signed up.
<?php endif ?>
```

The form is now wrapped inside an `if/else` block. Accessing the flash variables from a template is done through `$sf_user`. To test if the variable has been set, I have used the `hasFlash()` method, `$sf_user->hasFlash('Form')`. The `else` part of the statement contains the text rather than the form. Now if you submit your form, you will see the result as shown in the following screenshot:

We have now implemented an entire module for a user to sign up for our newsletter. Wouldn't it be really good if we could add this module to another application without all the copying, pasting, and fixing?

Creating a plugin

Symfony has many wonderful and time-saving features. But the two I am very fond of are the Symfony's plugin architecture and the currently increasing plugin repository.

It is always a good idea to create loosely coupled classes that can be integrated into other applications. In Symfony, not only should you follow this concept when coding, but also think of coding a module that you can use in another application. If you can manage this, then refactoring your module to a plugin will eventually save you many hours.

The signup module that we have created is fairly simple and straight forward, and is something which many sites do use. By refactoring our module and producing a plugin, you can install this plugin on any of your applications without having to rewrite any code.

Before we start, I think it's important that we have a look at the naming conventions. All the plugins available on the Symfony wiki follow the naming convention of sfPluginNamePlugin. Following this structure, I have made it a policy at Agile labs to name our plugins as alPluginNamePlugin. Also, a module-naming convention is important as we do not want to cause any conflicts with the modules already present in an application.

To help us in creating the plugin skeleton directory structure and to package the plugin, we are going to install `sfTaskExtraPlugin`. Go to the Symfony web site and download the plugin from `http://www.symfony-project.org/plugins/sfTaskExtraPlugin` to your hard disk. Once you have downloaded it, you can install it. I have downloaded the plugin to the `Documents` folder on my computer and to install it, I enter the following command:

```
$/home/timmy/workspace/milkshake>symfony plugin:install /home/timmy/
Documents/sfTaskExtraPlugin-0.0.1.tgz

$/home/timmy/workspace/milkshake>symfony cc
```

Remember that now we must enable this plugin before we can use it. Open up the project application file `config/ProjectConfiguration.clsss.php` and add the `sfTaskExtraPlugin` to the array using the following command:

```
$this->enablePlugins(array('sfPropelPlugin', 'DbFinderPlugin',
'sfTaskExtraPlugin'));
```

We can now start creating the directory structure for our plugin. Create a folder called `alSignupPlugin` in the `plugins/` folder. Just like an application, we can have modules within the plugin too. Hence, create a `modules/` folder inside the `alSignupPlugin` folder. Next, we can move our signup module folder `apps/frontend/modules/signup` that we created earlier to the new module folder that we just created. Once you have moved it, rename the folder from `signup` to `alSignup`.

 Be careful when copying entire folders to other locations when they are in subversion. Every folder will contain a hidden `.svn` folder. This will cause headaches later when you want to commit the code. To copy them, use the `svn export` command.

While we are creating folders, you can go ahead and create the `config/`, `data/` `data/fixtures`, `lib/`, `lib/forms/`, and `lib/model` folders in the `plugins/` `alSignupPlugin` directory. Your directory structure should reflect the following:

```
plugins/alSignupPlugin/config
                      /data
                      /data/fixtures
                      /lib
                      /lib/form
                      /lib/model
                      /test
```

There are nine steps in refactoring our module to a plugin. These are the steps:

1. A plugin can have its own schema, which is built after the main schema for the application. So we need to create a `schema.xml` file in the `plugins/orSignupPlugin/config` directory. We are then going to copy the schema code for the `newsletter_signups` and `newsletter_adverts` tables from the main `schema.xml` file, and place them in the plugin's `schema.xml` file. Because we have moved this, we delete this out of the main `schema` file. The following is how the plugin's `schema.xml` will look:

```xml
<?xml version="1.0" encoding="UTF-8"?>
<database name="propel" defaultIdMethod="native" noXsd="true"
        package="plugins.alSignupPlugin.lib.model">
  <table name="alsignup_newsletter_adverts" idMethod="native"
        phpName="AlSignupNewsletterAds">
    <column name="newsletter_adverts_id" type="INTEGER"
          required="true" autoIncrement="true"
          primaryKey="true" />
    <column name="advertised" type="VARCHAR" size="30"
          required="true" />
  </table>
  <table name="alsignup_newsletter_signups" idMethod="native"
        phpName="AlSignupNewsletterSignup">
    <column name="id" type="INTEGER" required="true"
          autoIncrement="true" primaryKey="true" />
    <column name="first_name" type="VARCHAR" size="20"
          required="true" />
    <column name="surname" type="VARCHAR" size="20"
          required="true" />
    <column name="email" type="VARCHAR" size="100"
          required="true" />
    <column name="activation_key" type="VARCHAR" size="100"
          required="true" />
    <column name="activated" type="BOOLEAN" default="0"
          required="true" />
```

```
    <column name="newsletter_adverts_id" type="INTEGER"
          required="true"/>
    <foreign-key foreignTable="alsignup_newsletter_adverts"
             onDelete="CASCADE">
       <reference local="newsletter_adverts_id"
                foreign="newsletter_adverts_id" />
    </foreign-key>
       <column name="created_at" type="TIMESTAMP" required="true" />
       <column name="updated_at" type="TIMESTAMP" required="true" />
    </table>
</database>
```

We have to make a few edits to the copied code in order to keep the naming convention in line with our plugin.

- ° The `package` attribute in the `<database>` tag needs to be changed from `lib.mobel` to `plugins.orSignupPlugin.lib.model`. When we build our models and forms, we want them to be placed in our plugin's `lib/` folder rather than that of the project. If you do not change this, when you build the models, they will be placed in the main `lib/model`. I have also changed the table names and the `phpName` (the models' name) to reflect the name of the plugin. This will prevent any naming conflicts. I have prefixed `alsignup_` to the table names and `AlSignup` to the `phpName`.

- ° I have had to change the `foreign_table` value to `alsignup_newsletter_adverts` to reflect the new table name.

Once this is in place, remove both the `newsletter_signups` and the `newsletter_` tables from the main `config/schema.xml` file.

2. Since we have just moved over the schema, let's also move over the fixtures. You will recall that we have data to populate the `newsletter_adverts` table, which is now called `alsignup_newsletter_adverts`. The fixtures file for a plugin works exactly the same as it does for the applications. We must create a `fixtures.yml` file in the `plugins/alSignupPlugin/data/fixtures/` folder. Once created, insert the following into it:

```
AlSignupNewsletterAds:
  nsa1:
    advertised: Internet Search
  nsa2:
    advertised: High Street
  nsa3:
    advertised: Poster
```

The model name has now changed from NewsletterAds to AlSignupNews-
letterAds to reflect the new model when we build it. Don't forget to remove
the old fixtures from the fixtures file.

3. Each plugin needs to have its own config.php file. This file is where we
    specify all the configuration settings for the plugin. As a plugin should be
    more or less plug and play, we have to add the plugin's routing rules to the
    start of the application's routing rules. In the plugins/alSignup/config/
    config.php file we configure our plugin to prepend the routing rules (which
    we will place in another file) only if the plugin is enabled as shown here:

```
if (sfConfig::get('app_alSignup_routes_register', true) &&
in_array('alSignup', sfConfig::get('sf_enabled_modules')))
{
  $this->dispatcher->connect('routing.load_configuration',
                   array('alSignupRouting',
                   'listenToRoutingLoadConfigurationEvent'));
}
```

We cannot just create a routing.yml file in the plugin because of the order
of the routing rules when loading. Therefore, we need to register an event
listener, routing.load_configuration, and prepend our rules to it. The
second argument passed in to the connect() method is an array. The first
argument of this array is the name of the class that handles the routing
rules and the second argument is the name of the function that holds
them, listenToRoutingLoadConfigurationEvent. Create a file called
alSignupRouting.php and store it in the plugin/alSignup/lib folder. This
file will hold our routing rules. Open the file and insert the following class:

```
class alSignupRouting
{
  /**
   * Listens to the routing.load_configuration event.
   *
   * @param sfEvent An sfEvent instance
   */
  static public function
  listenToRoutingLoadConfigurationEvent(sfEvent $event)
  {
    $r = $event->getSubject();

    // preprend our routes
    $r->prependRoute('signup', new sfRoute('/signup',
          array('module' => 'alSignup', 'action' => 'index')));
    $r->prependRoute('signup_submit', newsfRoute('/signup/submit',
          array('module' => 'alSignup', 'action' => 'submit')));
  }
}
```

As you can see, we have prepended each route to the application's routing rules. The first argument is the label, followed by a `sfRoute` object that is initialized with the URL, module, and action. Now that we have added the routing rules to our plugin, we can remove them from the `apps/frontend/config/routing.yml` file.

We can now go ahead and rebuild the models and forms by using the following pake task:

```
$/home/timmy/workspace/milkshake>symfony propel:build-all-load
--no-confirmation
```

```
$/home/timmy/workspace/milkshake>symfony cc
```

This will build our models and forms in the plugin's `lib/` folder and will insert the fixtures data back into the database for us.

4. After running the above tasks, you will notice that the new models and forms have been created for us. These new models reflect the change of table names in the schema. As we are now using models with a different name, we have to change the references to them in the action as well as in the form. Before we do this, we need to re-add a function to the newly created `AlSignupNewsletterAds` model. We created a `__toString()` function in the `NewsletterAds` model, which now needs to be transferred over to `AlSignupNewsletterSignup`. Open the `plugins/AlSignupPlugin/lib/model/AlSignupNewsletterSignup.php` file and add the following function:

```
public function __toString()
{
    return $this->getAdvertised();
}
```

As we do not need the `Newsletter` and the `NewsletterAds` models anymore, you can go ahead and delete them from the `lib/model`, `lib/model/om`, and `lib/model/map` folders as shown here:

```
rm -f lib/model/Newsl*
rm -f lib/om/BaseNewsl*
rm -f lib/map/NewsletterBuilder.php
```

5. With the models migrated over, we need to do the same with the form. If you look in the `plugin/alSignupPlugin/lib/form` directory, you will see that both the forms, `AlSignupNewsletterSignupForm` and `AlSignupNewsletterSignupForm`, have been created. First, you can delete `AlSignupNewsletterSignupAdsForm` and `BaseAlSignupNewsletterSignupAdsForm` as we do not need a form for this table. Next, open up the form that we initially created, `lib/form/NewsletterSignupForm.php`, and copy the code within the `configure()` method over to `plugin/alSignupPlugin/lib/form/AlSignupNewlsetterSignupForm`. Once that is done, you need make two changes. In both the widget and validator initialization, there is a reference to `NewsletterAds, 'newsletter_adverts_id' => new sfWidgetFormPropelChoice(array('model' => 'NewsletterAds'`. Here, change `NewsletterAds` to `AlSignupNewsletterAds` as this is now the name of the new model.

6. The final part of the migration is to amend the calls to the old `NewsletterSignupForm` within the action and rename the action class. Also, we have to change the configuration references to the `module.yml` file values that we had set for our email. Open the `action.class.php` file for the plugin located in the `plugins/alSignupPlugin/modules/actions` folder. First, change the action's class name from `SignupActions` to `alSignupActions`. At the moment, the action is instantiating the old form (which should have been deleted). Therefore, change both occurrences of

```
$this->form = new NewsletterSignupForm();
```

to:

```
$this->form = new AlSignupNewsletterSignupForm();
```

Next, we must amend the variables that we use to retrieve the values from the `module.yml` file that we had created earlier to hold the email values. I have amended them in the following code to reference the `alsignup` module, and not `signup`:

```
try{
        //Sendmail
        $transport = Swift_SendmailTransport::newInstance();
        $mailBody = $this->getPartial('activationEmail',
```

```
              array('name' => $this->form->getValue('first_name')));
      $mailer = Swift_Mailer::newInstance($transport);
      $message = Swift_Message::newInstance();
      $message->setSubject(sfConfig::get
                         ('mod_alsignup_mailer_subject'));
      $message->setFrom(array(sfConfig::get
        ('mod_alsignup_mailer_from_email') => sfConfig::get
                         ('mod_alsignup_mailer_from_name')));
      $message->setTo(array($this->form->getValue('email') =>
                         $this->form->getValue('first_name')));
      $message->setBody($mailBody, 'text/html');

      if(sfConfig::get('mod_alsignup_mailer_deliver'))
      {
         $result = $mailer->send($message);
      }
   }
}
```

We have now migrated the signup plugin to a reuseable plugin.

7. Next we perform housekeeping by deleting unneeded files and removing the old tables in the database, that is, all forms and filters.

8. We have now created our first plugin. But in order to use it, we must enable the plugin's module for the frontend application. We enable this in the `apps/frontend/config/settings.yml` file. In the `all` key, add the `enable_modules` parameter just as I have done here:

```
all:
  .settings:
    # Form security secret (CSRF protection)
    csrf_secret:        a15ba0eef94f781b04886f7453fe506d57feb431
# Unique secret to enable CSRF protection or false to disable

    # Output escaping settings
    escaping_strategy:       true           # Determines how
variables are made available to templates. Accepted values: on,
off.
    escaping_method:         ESC_SPECIALCHARS # Function or helper
used for escaping. Accepted values: ESC_RAW, ESC_ENTITIES, ESC_JS,
ESC_JS_NO_ENTITIES, and ESC_SPECIALCHARS.
    enabled_modules:         [default,alSignup]
```

9. Once that is all done, do not forget to clear the cache using the following command:

```
>symfony cc
```

If you have followed all of the aforementioned steps, then the plugin should now be active and working.

Packaging a plugin

There are three ways to include a plugin into our application:

- Copying a plugin into the plugin folder
- Using SVN externals to reference the plugin
- Using the Symfony `plugin:install` task to download and install the plugin

SVN externals are great and recommended, but sometimes it is easier to distribute your plugin as a package. This is very simple as the `sfTaskExtraPlugin` plugin that we had installed earlier comes with a `package` task.

First, add any additional information to the LICENCE and README files in the `alSignupPlugin` root directory. You can also modify the `package.xml.templ` file as this is the default template used to generate the `package.xml` file. When you are happy, run the following command:

```
>symfony plugin:package --plugin-version="0.1.0" alSignupPlugin
```

You will now be asked a few further questions, so fill them in. The output of this is shown in the following screenshot:

Summary

Symfony's form framework is another fantastic feature that helps developers with the tedious task of writing forms. Whether it is a Propel-based form or a simple form, creating forms and validating them is simple and rapid, not to mention more object orientated too. We created our own formatting class that produced a nice-looking prototype, and then progressed to create a fully-customized form.

We have seen how useful plugins are, but there is not a plugin for everything. Here we introduced you to Swift Mailer for sending out emails and integrated it into our application with a minimum effort, again showing you how Symfony can be expanded to use the other third-party libraries.

We then converted our signup module into a fully-working plugin. This demonstrated that when you build other web applications, you should write more generic and loosely coupled code so that it can be packaged up and reused in other projects.

5
Generating the Admin Area

So far we have built a fully-functional and dynamic Symfony application. We have not only coded parts, but have also used Symfony's CLI to generate our data models and clear the cache. Also, we have seen the use of plugins and even built our own.

Now that the frontend application is complete, we need a backend application so that we can add and modify content on the site.

In this chapter you will learn how to:

- Initialize the Propel admin generator
- Customize the initialized code
- Secure applications and actions based on credentials
- Work with foreign keys relationships within the generator

How Symfony can help us

When creating web sites, more often than not, the end users will require a backend application to edit parts of their site. This can sometimes lead to twice the amount of work depending on the requirements. One of Symfony's most important features is its generators. By initializing a Propel admin generator, an entire backend application based on the models can be created. What is more interesting is that the generated backend is highly customizable via a `generator.yml` file and is styled enough to be released, so that it can be deployed out-of-box. This file is responsible for configuring admin generator in most of its aspects.

There are two types of generators—initialized and generated. For the frontend, forms can be scaffolded, as with initialized or generated, whereas the administration can only be initialized. The main differences between the frontend scaffolding and the admin generator are:

- The templates generated by the admin generator are styled as a finished module. Scaffolded modules are not.

- Admin modules are customized through a configuration file. They can be easily extended using inheritance. Whereas, scaffolding is merely there to aid as a very useful starting point that contains the functionality to create, retrieve, edit, and delete (**CRUD**).

- Admin modules can be highly customized by the configuration file and can take advantage of pagination, filtering, and sorting.

- Scaffolding can be either initialized or generated. Whereas, the admin can only by initialized. We will look at both approaches later.

With all this in mind, we'll commence building our backend application using the admin generator.

Initializing generator

As the initialized admin generator modules are based on the existing models, generating the backend modules can only be done on a module basis. For example, if we want to create an administration module for the careers section, this would in fact create a whole careers module.

Creating application and module

Let's start by creating the backend application. Type the following in the terminal window:

```
> symfony generate:app --escaping-strategy=on --csrf-secret
                                        =UniqueSecret1 backend
```

This creates the backend application for us, which consists of the skeleton folder structure in the `apps/` folder and the backend controllers located in `web/backend. php` and `web/backend_dev.php`. This process is exactly the same as when you created the frontend application. And just like the frontend application, the backend has been built in the `app/` folder.

To add a new `StoreLocation` module to our application, type this in the terminal window:

```
> symfony propel:generate-admin backend StoreLocation
```

In this command:

- `propel:generate-admin` is a pake task that will initialize an admin module
- `backend` is the name of application that the module will be built in
- **Location** is the name of model that our module will be based on. Note that the name has to be exactly like model class name (`Location`)

Symfony will create a module using a `Location` model. In our example, a new module named `location` (lowercase) will be created in the `apps/backend/modules/` folder.

These few steps have created for us a backend application and a working module for the store locations. To see this in action, go to `http://milkshake/backend_dev.php/location` from your browser.

Exploring list view

If you have fixtures loaded (you should have), you will see a page with a records list. It will be similar to the list in the following screenshot:

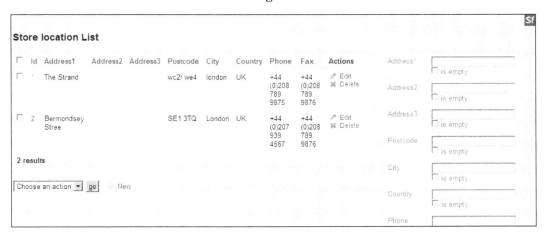

This is known as the **list view**. It is comprised of the record list, batch actions, and filtering options. The left half of the list view presents a list of records, and below the record list you will find a select box. This box is used to call actions for more than one record. In Symfony, this is called **batch actions**. By default we have only one batch action that will allow us to delete more records with one confirmation.

It is also very easy to write your own actions by adding their name into the `generator.yml` file and creating a new action in the `action.class.php` file.

The right half of the view list presents us with all available **filtering options**. The list view page is created by calling the automatically generated `executeIndex()` action and the `indexSuccess.php` template. If you click on the **New** link, you will see a nicely styled form (**edit view**) that will allow you to add new record.

Before we dive in too far, we should take a look at what exactly is happening underneath.

 If your backend area seems to be unstyled, please make sure you have a copy or an alias of the Symfony `sf` folder. This folder is located in Symfony's installation files in `data/web/sf`.

Looking into the generated list view code

By looking into the generated list view code, you will find out that the module `apps/backend/modules/store_location/actions/action.class.php` file actually doesn't contains any methods and the `apps/backend/modules/store_location/templates/` folder is empty. Before we can view any of the code that has been generated, we must first view the backend module in the browser. After the first request, the code for the module is generated in the `cache/env/` folder before it's parsed and the module is displayed. This is because the admin modules are only initialized, and not generated. Although the admin modules are only initialized, it means that we can use a configuration file to configure the module to our needs. We can also extend the generated base classes if we need non-standard and more sophisticated customization.

For this reason, admin modules cannot be generated. Only scaffolding, which is usually only for frontend applications, can be generated. This means that the module cannot be configured with a configuration file, and the generated code is the actual code that is not extending any parents or the framework.

If you take a look at the `cache/backend/dev/modules/` folder, you will see the following structure:

```
autoStore_location/actions/
  actions.class.php
autoStore_location/lib/
  BaseStore_locationGeneratorConfiguration.class.php
  BaseStore_locationGeneratorHelper.class.php
autoStore_location/templates/
  _assets.php
  editSuccess.php
  _filters_field.php
  _filters.php
  _flashes.php
  _form_actions.php
  _form_field.php
  _form_fieldset.php
  _form_footer.php
  _form_header.php
  _form.php
  indexSuccess.php
  _list_actions.php
  _list_batch_actions.php
  _list_field_boolean.php
  _list_footer.php
  _list_header.php
```

```
          _list.php
          _list_td_actions.php
          _list_td_batch_actions.php
          _list_td_stacked.php
          _list_td_tabular.php
          _list_th_stacked.php
          _list_th_tabular.php
          newSuccess.php
       _pagination.php
```

Notice how there are many partials? Each view is built up of several partials, which makes the structure flexible if you only want to edit only certain areas.

First, we will take a look at the `autoStore_location/actions/action.class.php`, which is the generated actions class. The following is the list of most important functions within actions:

Action	Description
executeIndex()	This action generates the first page we look at, which is a list of the records in the database. This file also calls a few internal functions that will generate filters, handle sorting, and pagination.
executeEdit()	This action generates the edit form.
executeNew()	This action generates the form for new items. It uses the same form object as executeEdit(), but allows us to customize the process of creating new objects.
executeUpdate()	This action handles updating of the form request. It uses the editSuccess template.
executeDelete()	This action handles the deletion.
executeBatch()	This action handles all batch actions.
executeBatchDelete()	This action is responsible for handling batch deletion.

There are also a few internally called methods that help in processing a form, creating pages, or sorting. Let's take a closer look at the automatically-generated `indexSuccess`:

```
public function executeIndex(sfWebRequest $request)
{
  // sorting
  if ($request->getParameter('sort'))
  {
    $this->setSort(array($request->getParameter('sort'),
                         $request->getParameter('sort_type')));
```

```
    }
    // pager
    if ($request->getParameter('page'))
    {
       $this->setPage($request->getParameter('page'));
    }

    $this->pager = $this->getPager();
    $this->sort = $this->getSort();
  }
```

This code is responsible for displaying the list view. It initializes a sorting method, rather than a pager. If you look into the getPager() method, you will also notice a code responsible for filtering and displaying paginated results.

 While it's not necessary to analyze all these automatically-generated methods, analyzing even a small part of them may, at some point, help you better understand how the admin generator works and what you can achieve with it. You should try to do this when you are more familiar with the basic admin generator possibilities.

As it was mentioned before, sooner or later we might need to either extend the above actions or customize them a little. But we cannot do so directly in the above files because they are stored in cache. To see the solution, we need to look in the apps/backend/modules/store_location folder. If we need to add, modify, or extend behavior, this is where all the modifications will go. As we progress through the chapter, you will see how this is done.

Let's look at one last point that concerns the routing. If we used the propel: generate-admin command as it was described earlier, routing will be created automatically in apps/backend/config/routing.yml:

```
store_location:
  class: sfPropelRouteCollection
  options:
    model:                StoreLocation
    module:               store_location
    prefix_path:          store_location
    column:               id
    with_wildcard_routes: true
```

As you can see in this code, routing is handled by the other class sfPropelRouteCollection. This class is handling all routes bound to our Propel StoreLocation model.

Customizing the admin generator

The configuration file for a backend module is the `generator.yml` file, which is located in the `apps/backend/modules/store_location/config` folder. Open up the `generator.yml` file for the `store_location` module. Surprisingly, the file is pretty sketchy.

```
generator:
  class: sfPropelGenerator
  param:
    model_class:           StoreLocation
    theme:                 admin
    non_verbose_templates: true
    with_show:             false
    singular:              ~
    plural:                ~
    route_prefix:          store_location
    with_propel_route:     1

    config:
      actions: ~
      fields:  ~
      list:    ~
      filter:  ~
      form:    ~
      edit:    ~
      new:     ~
```

The contents of the file specify the class that the module extends, along with the model and theme. What we will do first is customize the list view before moving on to the edit view. By default all of the columns of the `StoreLocation` model are displayed. We will tidy up the list by displaying only the `City`, `Country`, `Phone`, and `Fax` columns. I also want to remove all the filters as we don't need them in our applications. To customize the list view, all options must sit within the list parameter key. In the following code, I have added the list label and parameters as well as the code to disable filters:

```
generator:
  class: sfPropelGenerator
  param:
    model_class:           StoreLocation
    theme:                 admin
    non_verbose_templates: true
    with_show:             false
    singular:              ~
```

```
plural:              ~
route_prefix:        store_location
with_propel_route:   1

config:
  actions: ~
  fields:  ~
  list:
    title: Store Locations List
    display: [=city, country, phone, fax]
  filter:
    class: -
  form:    ~
```

When working with this file for the first time, care must be taken with spaces just like the amends we made to the `apps/frontend/config/settings.yml` file.

 If you use too many or too few spaces, or use tabs, either your modifications will not work or an error will occur.

In the code we just saw, the `list` attribute should be inline with the `actions`, `fields`, and `filter` attributes — this indentation is exactly six spaces. All further subparameters should be indented by another two spaces.

Let's look at the attributes under the `list` attribute:

Option	Description
title	This attribute sets the page heading.
display	This attribute has a list of all the columns that we would like to display. The column names defined here must match their equivalent column for the database table. I have appended an equals (=) sign to the city column. This will turn the city text into a link, which will link through to the edit form.

The following are the attributes under `filters`:

Option	Description
class	This parameter sets the handler class to one of classes inside `lib/filters/` `folder`. This way, we can define our own class to handle filters, or disable it by putting -, as an example.

After saving the `generator.yml` file, refresh the list view in your browser. You should see this:

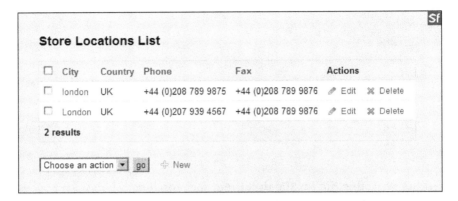

Please remember that if you are not using `_dev.php`, you will only see changes after clearing cache (by using the `symfony cc` command). It is recommended to always use the `dev` mode while developing your applications.

Customizing the edit view

Now that the list page is done, we can move on to the edit page. Without any modification, the page title will be set as **Edit Store Location**. What if we would like to add some dynamic text from database? We can easily do that:

```
list:
  title:  Store Locations
  display: [=city, country, phone, fax]
filter:
  class: -
form:    ~
edit:
  title:  Edit Location for: %%city%%
new:      ~
```

The `title` sub key sets the title on the form just like it does in the list view, but this time we have added a `city` column name surrounded by double percent signs. This tells Symfony that it has to display information about the city of the currently loaded database object. After entering into the edit view, you should see this:

Handling foreign keys using admin generator

Back in Chapter 3, *Adding the Business Logic and Complex Application Logic*, we had to display the locations for each vacancy. This was very simple to achieve by using the proxy methods. Using the `generator.yml` configuration file, working with foreign keys is just as easy. Moving on to the vacancies module, we create it in the exact same way. But this time we give the module a new name, and not the name suggested by the model name.

```
> symfony propel:generate-admin --module="vacancies" backend Vacancy
```

As you can see, there is an optional parameter — `module=""` that will allow us to name our module on our own. Before we continue to view our vacancies module, we must add a `__toString()` method to the `StoreLocation` model in `lib/model/StoreLocation.php`:

```
class StoreLocation extends BaseStoreLocation
{
  public function __toString()
  {
    return $this->getCity(). ' (' . $this->getCountry() .')';
  }
}
```

Add the following code to `data/fixtures/fixtures.yml`:

```yaml
StoreLocation:
  l1:
    address1: The Strand
    address2:
    postcode: wc2r we4
    city: london
    country: UK
    phone: +44 (0)208 789 9875
    fax: +44 (0)208 789 9876
  l2:
    address1: Bermondsey Stree
    address2:
    postcode: SE1 3TQ
    city: London
    country: UK
    phone: +44 (0)207 939 4567
    fax: +44 (0)208 789 9876
Vacancy:
  va1:
    position: Chief
    position_description: |
      Calling all shakers to Milkshake..
      Must shake shakes and work the till
    location_id: l1
    closing_date: 2008-09-09
```

After adding the code, reload the fixtures with this command:

```
>symfony propel:data-load
```

Now we are ready. If you look at the new `vacancies` module in your web browser at
`http://milkshake/backend_dev.php/vacancies`, you will see:

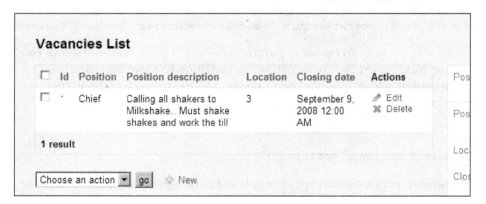

Now click on the number in the **Id** column to edit the record:

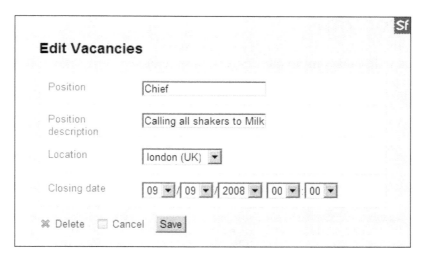

Notice how the location in the list view are presented by its foreign key under the Locations column. But on edit view, they are presented by the results of the StoreLocation __toString() method. We need to alter our generator.yml code inside backend/modules/vacancies/config. Using this opportunity, we also remove filters because we don't need them:

```
list:
    display: [=position, store_location, closing_date]
filter:
    class: -
```

We need to do that because the list view is showing us the value from the location_id column (from the vacancies table), whereas the edit view is connected to a form object and is presenting us a select box widget with all the StoreLocation items. To make the list view to do the same, we have to inform it about the object we want to display (store_location). Of course, not every relation can be represented in that way.

Accessing application settings from generator.yml

You can set the `fields` parameter key to parameters for individual fields by adding what field you want to modify as a parameter key, and passing it to the appropriate parameters.

```
config:
  actions: ~
  fields:
    store_location:
      label: 'Location'
    position_description:
      label: 'Description'
      help: 'Describe a position'
  list:
    display: [=position, store_location, closing_date]
```

Going down the list:

Field	Description
store_location	The `label` attribute allows you to set the label name on the template. We want to name the column in the same way as it is presented in the edit view (`Location`).
position_ description	We change the label in this field to `Description`. The `help` parameter allows us to add some hint for administrator that will show up under the input field.

In the next chapter, we will take a look into a way of creating more advanced fields, changing their types by customizing widgets, and adding more advanced JavaScript features.

Finally, clear the cache and take a look at the edit form. It should look similar to this:

We now have to adjust the list view to show the position, location, and closing date.

Using partials in the generated views

Although the generator is good, there are some limitations if you want to display some more complicated information or present it differently. Let's just say we need to mark all the old closing dates in bold and red color, and also change the date format to d/m/y.

We cannot do all of that inside the generator.yml file; instead, we can use partials. We have to make a small modification to the generator.yml file and create a new partial.

First, we'll modify the generator.yml file to this:

```
fields:
  store_location:
    label: 'Location'
  position_description:
    label: 'Description'
    help: 'Describe a position'
list:
  display: [=position, store_location, _closing_date]
```

Partials start with an underscore. It is OK to have partials named differently than our database column names. But if you use a partial to present database columns, you will still have sorting options. Adding the name of the partial to the list of columns that we want to display is all that is needed. In our application we have added _closing_date, which will be displayed after the location. Next, we have to create the partial. All templates are located within the module's template folder. Therefore, we have to create the partial to the apps/backend/modules/vacancies/templates folder, naming it _closing_date.php. Once the partial is created, open the file and add the following code snippet:

```php
<?php if (strtotime($vacancy->getClosingDate()) < time()): ?>
  <span style="color: red; font-weight: bold;">
    <?php echo $vacancy->getClosingDate('d/m/Y'); ?>
  </span>
<?php else: ?>
  <?php echo $vacancy->getClosingDate('d/m/Y'); ?>
<?php endif; ?>
```

The admin generator in the list view uses the $vacancy object, so we can use its proxy method to access the related date. Now that everything is in place, clear the cache and revisit the vacancy list view at http://milkshake/backend_dev.php/vacancies.

Customizing the layout

The only thing left to do for the layout is to add the navigation and style it a little. Therefore, open apps/backend/templates/layout.php.

We'll add the following to produce the navigation:

```
<!DOCTYPE html PUBLIC "-//W3C//DTD XHTML 1.0 Transitional//EN"
"http://www.w3.org/TR/xhtml1/DTD/xhtml1-transitional.dtd">
<html xmlns="http://www.w3.org/1999/xhtml" xml:lang="en" lang="en">
  <head>
    <?php include_http_metas() ?>
    <?php include_metas() ?>
    <?php include_title() ?>
    <link rel="shortcut icon" href="/favicon.ico" />
    <style type="text/css">

      #top_menu {
        padding: 10px 0;
      }

      #top_menu a {
        font-family: arial, helvetica, clean, sans-serif;
        text-decoration: none;
        font-size: 14px;
      }
```

```
      #top_menu a:hover {
        text-decoration: underline;
      }
    </style>
  </head>
  <body>
    <div id="top_menu">
      <?php echo link_to('Store Locations', '@store_location') ?> |
      <?php echo link_to('Vacancies', '@vacancy') ?>
    </div>
    <?php echo $sf_content ?>
  </body>
</html>
```

Next, open the apps/backend/config/view.yml file and amend the settings as shown in the following code snippet:

```
default:
  http_metas:
    content-type: text/html

  metas:
    title:         Milkshake Administration
    robots:        noindex, nofollow
    description:
    keywords:
    language:      en

  stylesheets:     []

  javascripts:     []

  has_layout:      on
  layout:          layout
```

Securing the application

Finally, we must secure the backend application with an authentication mechanism. We will accomplish this by installing the sfGuardPlugin plugin to provide us with the improved auth process and login actions, and then setting the security settings of the application.

Just like any other PHP application, security settings are generally stored in the session. Symfony transparently handles this within the sfUser class along with any other session data.

Setting and retrieving attributes in the session is similar to accessing any other parameter holder.

```
$this->getUser()->setAttribute('attribute');
$this->getUser()->getAttribute('attribute', 'default_value');
$this->getUser()->hasAttribute('attribute');
```

Of course, accessing session attributes from the template is similar to this:

```
$sf_user->getAttribute('attribute');
```

By default, sessions are stored in files on the server. But just by modifying the `apps/backend/config/factories.yml` file, you can configure Symfony's session handling behavior to store sessions in a database, set the session timeout, set the Symfony cookie name, and more.

To make our application secure, we can use a mixture of two methods. You can either let an authenticated user use the actions, or fine-tune the user access using credentials. For the purpose of our application, the latter would normally do. But we will exaggerate the user base to allow a non-admin level account, with no deletion privileges or access to the user accounts menu.

Moving on to secure the backend application, you must install the `sfGuardPlugin` (`http://www.symfony-project.org/plugins/sfGuardPlugin`). To do that, you should follow the installation instructions from the **Readme** tab. Once the plugin is installed, follow the readme guide to set up the plugin.

Please enable all modules and set `secure:` on for our backend application.

After following all the instructions, remember to repopulate the database with the following command:

```
> symfony propel:data-load
```

 When this book was written, there was no `sfGuardPlugin` for Symfony 1.3 and so the install task was failing. However, it was possible to download the version dedicated for Symfony 1.2, unpack it into the `plugins/` folder, and then proceed with the normal installation procedure from readme.

Make sure you have your user added with the `symfony guard:create-user` command and enable all modules in the backend in `backend/config/settings.yml`.

```
all:
  .settings:
    enabled_modules: [default, sfGuardGroup, sfGuardUser,
sfGuardPermission, sfGuardAuth]
```

After installation, refresh the screen and you should see a login screen similar to this:

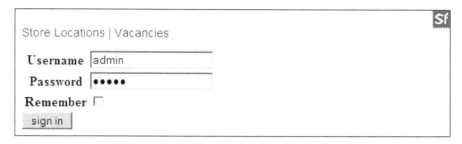

As you can see, the menu is still visible. To avoid that, we have to change our `layout.php` file in the `backend/template` folder:

```
<body>
  <?php if ($sf_user->isAuthenticated()): ?>
  <div id="top_menu">
    <?php echo link_to('Store Locations', '@store_location') ?> |
    <?php echo link_to('Vacancies', '@vacancy') ?>
  </div>
  <?php endif; ?>
  <?php echo $sf_content ?>
```

The `isAuthenticated()` method is checked whenever the user is logged in. Now, we should log in using the login/password of the user we created with the `symfony guard:create-user` command.

With `sfGuard` in place, we can now add permissions, permission groups, and users. Browse to `http://milkshake/backend_dev.php/sf_guard_permission`. Add the permissions to update, edit, delete, and admin. Next, we can create a group that will contain these permissions. Let's create a group called `admin`, which encompasses all the permissions and another group called `updater`, which does not include the delete or admin permission. To access the group permissions, browse to `http://milkshake/backend_dev.php/sf_guard_group`. The following screenshot shows creating the `updater` group:

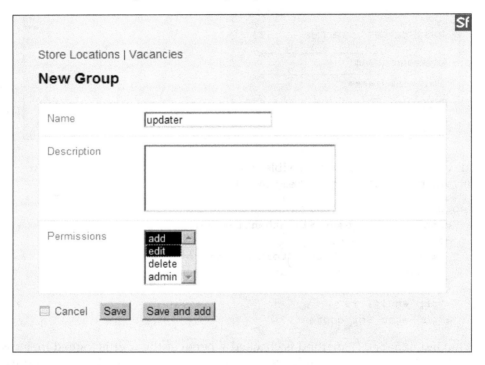

We add the user that you just created to the `admin` group and now create a second user account. Browse to `http://milkshake/backend_dev.php/sf_guard_user` and edit your user by adding him/her to the `admin` group, and another user assigned to updater.

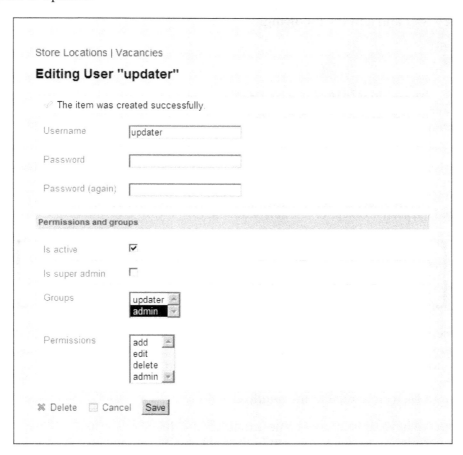

Now that we have users associated to groups and permissions, we can set up the security settings.

Setting up credentials (permissions)

There are two ways that we can add credentials—either on a module/action basis or on an application/action basis. For our backend application, we will use a mixture of both application-wide and action-based credentials. Open `apps/backend/config/security.yml` and add the following:

```
default:
    is_secure: on

#Set the credentials for the delete action
delete:
    credentials:      [delete]
```

Setting `is_secure` to `on` in the applications `security.yml` file means that a user must be logged in to access anything in the application. The `delete` parameter key refers to the action, which in our case is the delete action. Here we have set `credentitals` to `delete`, which means that the user must have the `delete` credential in order to execute the delete action.

> **Remember**: The delete action is not the only action that can remove items. We also delete batch actions using the delete action, and if you want to protect your application, you also have to remember about batch actions.

Of course, this solution fits our model. If your application contains many modules with many different actions, it might be a better idea to add the security settings to each module/action. This means that in every module you will need to create a `security.yml` file in the `apps/application/module/config` folder path. Then, of course, add each credential to the required actions.

Although we have only allowed a user that has the delete credential associate to their account permission to delete an item in the backend, Symfony can cater for a more complex credential criteria. For example, if we wanted to allow a user who has the edit and admin permission to delete an item, we could use this:

```
#Set the credentials for the delete action
delete:
    credentials:      [[delete, admin]]
```

This allows the delete action to be executed by a user with the credentials of either `delete` *or* admin.

However, the following command would allow the delete action to be executed by a user with both the credentials of delete *and* edit, or by a user with the admin credential:

```
#Set the credentials for the delete action
delete:
  credentials:      [[[delete, edit], admin]]
```

Handling credentials in templates

Now that we have the sfGuardPlugin working, the administrator of the site will at some point want to add or delete users. We'll add the remaining items to the navigation as follows:

```
<body>
  <?php if ($sf_user->isAuthenticated()): ?>
  <div id="top_menu">
    <?php echo link_to('Store Locations', '@store_location') ?> |
    <?php echo link_to('Vacancies', '@vacancy') ?>
    <?php echo link_to('Users', '@sf_guard_user') ?> |
    <?php echo link_to('Groups', '@sf_guard_group') ?> |
    <?php echo link_to('Permissions', '@sf_guard_permission') ?> |
    <?php echo link_to('Logout', '@sf_guard_signout') ?>
  </div>
  <?php endif; ?>
  <?php echo $sf_content ?>
```

Although this will help and allow the administrator to navigate around the backend, there is one flaw. Anyone who is authenticated can access the sfGuard plugin to edit accounts. This flaw is very simple to rectify by following these steps:

1. We'll lock down the sfGuard modules. Create a security.yml file in the plugins/sfGuardPlugin/modules/sfGuardUser/config folder and then add:

```
default:
  credentials:      [admin]
```

2. Once you have done that, copy the newly created security.yml file to the config folders of the sfGuardGroup and sfGuardPermission modules. This means that a user's account must have the admin permission to access each of the modules.

3. We can access the session ($sf_user) from the template to check if the user is authenticated and also if their account has the admin credential. Therefore, add this to the layout.php file:

```
<body>
  <?php if ($sf_user->isAuthenticated()): ?>
  <div id="top_menu">
    <?php echo link_to('Store Locations', '@store_location') ?> |
    <?php echo link_to('Vacancies', '@vacancy') ?> |
  <?php if ($sf_user->hasCredential('admin')): ?>
      <?php echo link_to('Users', '@sf_guard_user') ?> |
      <?php echo link_to('Groups', '@sf_guard_group') ?> |
    <?php echo link_to('Permissions', '@sf_guard_permission') ?> |
  <?php endif; ?>
    <?php echo link_to('Logout', '@sf_guard_signout') ?>
  </div>
  <?php endif; ?>
  <?php echo $sf_content ?>
```

As you can see, we have wrapped the navigation inside another if statement. The inner if statement checks to see if the authenticated user has the admin credential. Of course if both statements are true then the user is in fact both authenticated and is an admin. If however the authenticated user is not an admin, then the sfGuard modules are not shown.

Tidying up the backend

Through out the chapter, we have managed to create and secure an entire backend application. But before we commit our work, we have a few small vanity amends that need to be done to tidy up the interface. They are:

1. Forward the homepage URL to one of the modules.
2. Style the login form and permissions template.

After you have done that, commit the code to svn. But before committing, add the svn:ignore tag to all the folders under the cache folder.

Summary

In this chapter we have learned how to use the Symfony admin generator, initialize it, and then configure and customize it so that it can fit our needs. We have also taken some time to secure our application and familiarize with the Symfony credential system. All these Symfony features have helped us to write the admin panels in a much quicker and easier way than before. The admin generator is one of the most important features of Symfony framework because it can help save time, and free us from doing the basic and mostly boring tasks.

6
Advanced Forms and JavaScript

So far we have built frontend and backend web applications. You have seen and used many wonderful features that Symfony has to offer. Of course, Symfony not only helps developers with server-side scripting, but also provides helpers and widgets for client-side scripting. As mentioned in the earlier chapters, the Symfony framework also encompasses other projects such as Propel. Therefore, it makes sense to do the same when it comes to client-side scripting.

In this chapter you will learn how to:

- Add JavaScript code into your Symfony project
- Create a more advanced admin area by adding more advanced widgets and handling many-to-many relations
- Add an autocomplete feature using the `JQueryAutoComplete` widget

Adding JavaScript code into the Symfony project

JavaScript is something that modern web sites can't live without. It allows us to create amazing effects, or just make a page visitor's life easier. This section will show us how Symfony can make a developer's life easier by providing some enhancements and helpers to make work simple.

JavaScript frameworks

Amazingly, there are some developers out there who are still coding a lot of unneeded JavaScript from scratch. Although there is nothing wrong with this, there are easy alternatives. Just like Symfony is a PHP framework, there are many good JavaScript frameworks available as well. Here is a list of a few such frameworks:

- Prototype
- JQuery
- Mootools
- YUI (Yahoo! User Interface Library)
- Dojo

Not only do these frameworks make coding JavaScript simple, but they can also be efficiently extended with add-ons and/or plugins. Not to mention that they are also cross-browser compatible. For example, I generally use JQuery, and looking at the JQuerysite (`http://www.jquery.com`), you can see that there are hundreds of plugins readily available that provide a great deal of complete modules that work out of the box. Similarly, Prototype, for example, has script.aculo.us that extends the Prototype framework to add visual effects.

Using JavaScript helpers

Adding JavaScript to a template means that the JavaScript code must reside between the HTML `<script>` tags:

```
<script type="text/javascript">
//<![CDATA[

//]]>
</script>
```

But when using Symfony, such coding blocks are handled within the helpers. For example, adding the above code to a page as well as a function using Symfony's JavaScript helper is as simple as this:

```
<?php use_helper('JavascriptBase'); ?>
<?php echo javascript_tag("
   function name()
   {
      //Code
   }
") ?>
```

Another way of adding JavaScript to a page is to link an external JavaScript file. To do so, we would normally add this:

```
<script type="text/javascript" src="mysscipt.js"></script>
```

But using the `javascript_include_tag` helper would mean we could write the following:

```
<?php echo javascript_include_tag('myscript') ?>
```

Note that I have purposely left off the suffix `.js`. This is because Symfony will automatically add it for you. Also, if the script resides in the `/js` directory, then the suffix will be added for you too.

Adding JavaScript files into the header section

It is simple to add JavaScript code to individual templates, but what if you want to add a JavaScript within the header of a page, or several pages, or a certain JavaScript depending on the action?

One way would be to use the tags mentioned earlier in the templates layout and wrap the JavaScripts in the `if` statements. The only problem with this is that it can look messy. A better way is to place the required JavaScript filenames in the module's `view.yml` file or the application's `view.yml` file for a global include. For example, if you open the application's `apps/frontend/config/view.yml` configuration file, you will find:

```
default:
  http_metas:
    content-type: text/html

  metas:
    #title:         symfony project
    #description:   symfony project
    #keywords:      symfony, project
    #language:      en
    #robots:        index, follow

  stylesheets:     [main.css]

  javascripts:     []

  has_layout:      on
  layout:          layout
```

At the moment, the `javascripts` parameter key is empty. But if we were to add:

```
javascripts:          [myscript, myotherscript]
```

then Symfony will add the scripts to the response and place the script within the head. If we wanted to use only one of the global JavaScripts plus another script in one of our templates, we could add to the following to the module's configuration file, `view.yml`:

```
javascripts:          [-myscript, myotherscript, thisscript]
```

The minus sign in front of `myscript` means that this will be removed and thus, the global configuration will not load it.

Another way in which you can add a JavaScript is within the action by adding it to the response as follows:

```
$this->getResponse()->addJavascript('myscript');
```

When adding JavaScript to the `view.yml` file or to the response object, the template must have a `<head></head>` section. This is because the scripts are added just before the closing `<head>` tag (`</head>`). If there is no `</head>` tag, the scripts will not be added.

When using any of the JavaScript features that we will cover, you must explicitly declare the JavaScript helper on the template like this:

`<?php use_helper('JavaScriptBase')?>`

Else, add the JavaScript helper into the `standard_helpers` section within the application's `config/settings.yml` file.

Creating more advanced admin modules

In this section, we will add another admin module that will allow us to add new milkshakes. This module is more advanced than the modules we have used so far. To make this admin module more user-friendly, we should consider:

- Allowing image files to be uploaded and thumbnails to be automatically generated
- Hiding the `thumbnail_url` field, as we don't need to display this
- Adding a preview of the uploaded image file
- Making a milkshake flavor list easier to use

Installing the required plugins and libraries

In most cases when we are dealing with forms, we use dedicated Symfony form objects and their widgets to do the job. In such situations, using helpers as previously described may be very difficult as we would have to render each and every field ourselves.

Symfony, by default, comes without any widget that requires an external library or framework. However, some of the most popular widgets (that were bundled as normal helpers in Symfony 1.0) are now packed into a plugin named `sfFormExtraPlugin`. To use these widgets, we have to install this plugin first:

```
> symfony plugin:install sfFormExtraPlugin
```

This plugin contains very useful widgets, but all of them require some additional libraries. Therefore, the developers decided to not add these widgets to Symfony's core.

The following table presents a list of widgets that are added with `sfFormExtraPlugin`:

Plugin name	Description
`sfWidgetFormJQueryAutocompleter` `sfWidgetFormPropelJQueryAutocompleter`	Displays an input box with autocomplete support using JQuery library. The second widget also integrates with Propel.
`sfWidgetFormJQueryDate`	A nicely formatted date picker using the JQuery and JQueryUI libraries.
`sfWidgetFormPropelChoiceGrouped` `sfWidgetFormDoctrineChoiceGrouped`	The Propel and Doctrine widgets for using with many-to-many relations.
`sfWidgetFormReCaptcha`	The Captcha widget for Symfony.
`sfWidgetFormSelectDoubleList`	A very nice plugin that helps us to handle many-to-many relations.
`sfWidgetFormTextareaTinyMCE`	A widget that helps us in adding the TinyMCE WYSIWYG editor into form.

Some of widgets listed in the table require additional JavaScript libraries to be installed. In this chapter, we will need three additional libraries:

- JQuery (http://jquery.com/) — version 1.3.2
- JQuery UI (http://jqueryui.com/) — version 1.7.1
- TinyMCE (http://tinymce.moxiecode.com/) — version 3.4.2.1

Next to the URLs, I have given information about the latest stable versions that were available while writing this book. Widgets, of course, should work with the newer versions too, but the JQuery UI library often requires a specific JQuery branch to work properly. (For example, JQuery UI version 1.7.1 requires JQuery 1.3.)

Both JQuery and JQuery UI can be unpacked directly into the `web/js` directory (I have also moved UI stylesheets into the Symfony `/web/css` directory) or into any subdirectory (say, `web/js/jquery`). The TinyMCE package should be accessible from `web/js/tiny_mce/tiny_mce.js`.

Please remember to add the libraries into the `view.yml` configuration file. We should have `view.yml` modified to have the code similar to this:

```
stylesheets:    [smoothness/jquery-ui-1.7.1.custom.css]
javascripts:    [jquery-1.3.2.min.js,
                jquery-ui.1.7.1.custom.min.js,
                tiny_mce/tiny_mce.js]
```

This modification can be added either to the global `view.yml` file or to the module's `view.yml` file in which you really need these libraries.

Next, we have to install `sfThumbnailPlugin`:

```
> symfony plugin:install sfThumbnailPlugin
```

This plugin will provide us with easy methods for creating image thumbnails. It supports both the GD and ImageMagick PHP modules.

After installing the plugins, please remember to enable them in the project's configuration file, clear the cache (`symfony cc`), and publish the assets (`symfony plugin:publish`).

By the time this book was written, both plugins were not officially released for Symfony 1.3. However, it was possible to download plugins for version 1.2 manually, and use them in version 1.3.

Creating an advanced admin module

It's time to show some practical usage of the libraries that we just installed. Let's make a new backend module for our milkshake model:

```
symfony propel:generate-admin --module="milkshakes" backend Milkshake
```

Before we can use that module, we have to modify our `milkshakes` and `milkshake_flavor` tables to enable Symfony's magic with M-N (many-to-many) relations. We have to modify the `schema.xml` file as follows:

```
<table name="milkshakes" idMethod="native" phpName="Milkshake">
  <column name="id" type="INTEGER" required="true"
          autoIncrement="true" primaryKey="true" index="true" />
  <column name="name" type="VARCHAR" size="100"
          required="true" index="true"  />
  <column name="image_url" type="VARCHAR" size="255"
          required="true" />
  <column name="thumb_url" type="VARCHAR" size="255"
          required="true" />
```

We have now updated the allowed the `varchar` size to `255`. We also need to modify the `milkshake_flavor` table as follows:

```
<table name="milkshake_flavors" phpName="MilkshakeFlavor">
  <column name="milkshake_id" primaryKey="true"
          type="INTEGER" required="true" />
  <column name="flavor_id" primaryKey="true"
          type="INTEGER" required="true" />
  <foreign-key foreignTable="flavors" onDelete="CASCADE">
    <reference local="flavor_id" foreign="id" />
  </foreign-key>
  <foreign-key foreignTable="milkshakes" onDelete="CASCADE">
    <reference local="milkshake_id" foreign="id" />
  </foreign-key>
</table>
```

Here, we first removed the Primary Key column `id` and then added the `primaryKey="true"` expression into both the Foreign Key columns. To enable these changes, we also have to rebuild models, forms, and filters by typing:

```
> symfony propel:build-all-load
```

Now, we have to make sure that the `Flavor` class has the `__toString()` method. The following are the required modifications for the `lib/model/Flavor.php` file:

```
class Flavor extends BaseFlavor
{
  public function __toString()
  {
    return $this->getName();
  }
}
```

These changes are required because of the already created relations between the flavor and milkshake models.

> Each time we have any relation in a Propel object (regardless of whether it's a one-to-many or many-to-many relation), we have to add the __toString() method. This is to inform Symfony about what it should display when it will be accessing a class object within relation.

After creating the module and going into the edit view (from `http://milkshake/ backend_dev.php/milkshakes`, where you can edit any item), you should see something similar to this screenshot:

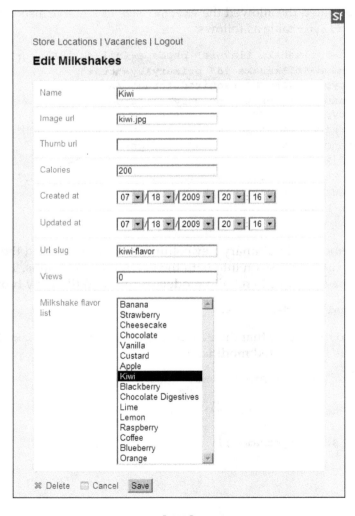

Adding file upload and thumbnails

First, we are going to add an upload feature and an automatic thumbnail creation. To do this, we have to modify the MilkshakeForm class in lib/form/MilkshakeForm.class.php by adding the following code:

```
class MilkshakeForm extends BaseMilkshakeForm
{
  public function configure()
  {
    // removing fields we don't want to display
    unset($this['thumb_url']);
    unset($this['views']);

    // setting image_url as input type="file"
    $this->widgetSchema['image_url'] = new sfWidgetFormInputFile();

    // setting validator for file upload
    $this->validatorSchema['image_url'] = new sfValidatorFile(array
            ('path' => sfConfig::get('sf_upload_dir').'/milkshakes',
             required' => true));
  }
}
```

The easiest way to add a thumbnail creation is to override the setImageUrl() method in the Milkshake class located under lib/model/Milkshake.php, as presented here:

```
class Milkshake extends BaseMilkshake
{
  public function setUrlSlug($v)
  {
    //Remove all non-alphanumeric characters except for a space.
    $newV = preg_replace('/\s+/', '-', $v);
    $newV = preg_replace('/[^a-zA-Z0-9\-]/', '', $newV);
    // trim and lowercase
    $newV = strtolower(trim($newV, '-'));
    return parent::setUrlSlug($newV);
  }
  public function setImageUrl($value)
  {
    // taking upload path from config
    $uploadPath = sfConfig::get('sf_upload_dir').'/milkshakes/';
    $thumbPrefix = 'thumb_';
    // removing old thumbnail
    $oldImage = $this->getImageUrl();

    if (!empty($oldImage)
      && is_file($uploadPath.$thumbPrefix.$oldImage))
```

```
  {
    unlink($uploadPath.$thumbPrefix.$oldImage);
  }
  // creating thumbnail
  if (!empty($value) && is_file($uploadPath.$value))
  {
    // creating thumbnail
    $thumb = new sfThumbnail(80, 60, true, false, 90);
    $thumb->loadFile($uploadPath.$value);
    $thumb->save($uploadPath.$thumbPrefix.$value);

    // rescaling.
    $rescale = new sfThumbnail(950, 580, true, false, 100);
    $rescale->loadFile($uploadPath.$value);
    $rescale->save($uploadPath.$value);
  }
  parent::setImageUrl($value);
  parent::setThumbUrl($thumbPrefix.$value);
  }
}
```

This will provide us with an automatically generated thumbnail and save the thumbnail's filename into the `thumb_url` column of our database. Uploaded files will be placed in the `web/uploads/milkshakes` subdirectory.

Now we have to display the thumbnail we created. To do so, we should add a new partial into the `apps/backend/modules/milkshakes/templates/_thumb.php` file with the following code:

```
<?php if ($form->getObject()->getThumbUrl()): ?>
<div class="sf_admin_form_row sf_admin_text
    sf_admin_form_field_image_url">
  <div>
    <label for="milkshake_image_url">Image preview</label>
    <?php echo image_tag('/uploads/milkshakes/'.
                        $form->getObject()->getThumbUrl()
    ); ?>
  </div>
</div>
<?php endif; ?>
```

 In edit view, we do not have direct access to the Propel object, but we do have access to the form object. To get a Propel object, we have to use the `getObject()` form method.

Handling many-to-many relations

As you may remember from the previous chapters, the `milkshakes` table in our database is related to the `milkshake_flavor` table with many-to-many relations. Symfony can handle these relations very easily, but the default way of showing them is not very good for lists with many records. Symfony will simply create a multiple-select control.

Lucky for us, the developers predicted such needs and created which is able to have a different `render_class`. The plugin `sfFormExtraPlugin` contains a render class for this plugin called `sfWidgetFormSelectDoubleList`. To enable it, we should modify our `MilkshakeForm` class and add the following code:

```
// setting image_url as input type="file"
$this->widgetSchema['image_url'] = new sfWidgetFormInputFile();

// setting AdminDoubleList View
$this->widgetSchema['milkshake_flavor_list']
  ->setOption('renderer_class', 'sfWidgetFormSelectDoubleList');
```

That's it! After refreshing this page, you should see something similar to the following screenshot:

You may not see the image thumbnail until you re-upload your images within the admin areas, as the previously created images were located in the images/ directory, and not in uploads/milkshakes/.

Adding jQuery calendar and TinyMCE widget

Let's get back to the vacancies module for a while. We could add two more improvements to it:

- We could make choosing closing dates a little easier
- We could add a WYSIWYG editor for a description field

Lucky for us, both tasks are very easy if you have installed JQuery UI and Tiny MCE. To make both the changes possible, we simply have to add the following code into lib/form/ VacancyForm.class.php:

```php
public function configure()
{
  // setting closing_date as calendar widget
  $this->widgetSchema['closing_date'] = new
                              sfWidgetFormJQueryDate();

  // adding TinyMCE widget
  $this->widgetSchema['position_description'] =
    new sfWidgetFormTextareaTinyMCE(array(
                  'width' => '500', 'height' => '150'));
}
```

The results will be similar to the next screenshot:

To complete our work on the backend, we should add a newly created module into navigation and tidy up the list view, as we did in Chapter 5.

Autocompleting the search

To demonstrate how simple it is to use the JavaScript form widgets, we are going to add an autocomplete search form at the top of the menu page. After a user starts typing in the search box, results will be displayed on key up even before he/she clicks on the "search" button.

To complete this task, we will use a widget called sfWidgetFormPropelJQueryAutocompleter. This widget is very useful when we are dealing with a Propel object and need an autocomplete feature.

First, we need to create a new search form. Create the
`lib/form/MilkshakeSearchForm.class.php` file and add the
following code to it:

```php
<?php
class MilkshakeSearchForm extends sfForm
{
  public function configure()
  {
    $this->setWidgets(array
                ('url_slug' => new sfWidgetFormChoice(array
                  ('choices' => array(),'renderer_class' =>
                    'sfWidgetFormJQueryAutocompleter',
                    'renderer_options' =>
                      array('url' => '/menu/search',),
      ))
    ));
    $this->widgetSchema->setFormFormatterName('div');
  }
}
?>
```

This code will create a form with an autocomplete field. Data for that field will be
delivered in the JSON format through the /menu/search action. The widget will
pass two parameters to that URL—limit and q. limit will have the maximum
allowed records, while q will have the word given by user. Now, we need to create
an appropriate action in the apps/frontend/menu/actions/action.class.php file:

```php
public function executeSearch(sfWebRequest $request)
  {
    $this->getResponse()
      ->setContentType('application/json');
    $milkshakes = MilkshakePeer::searchMilkshakesAjax(
      $request->getParameter('q'), $request->getParameter('limit')
    );
    return $this->renderText(json_encode($milkshakes));
  }
```

This action generates an output for widget control. As you can see, the results are
obtained from the MilkshakePeer::searchMilkshakesAjax() method. This
method should have a code similar to the following:

```php
public static function searchMilkshakesAjax($q, $limit)
  {
    $c = new Criteria();
    $c->add(self::NAME, '%'.$q.'%', Criteria::LIKE);
    $c->addAscendingOrderByColumn(self::NAME);
```

```
    $c->setLimit($limit);
    $milkshakes = array();
    foreach (self::doSelect($c) as $milkshake)
    {
       $milkshakes[$milkshake->getUrlSlug()] = $milkshake->getName();
    }

    return $milkshakes;
  }
```

This method is simply taking all of the results for a given parameter q and returning an array indexed by UrlSlug. The autocomplete method will return an index when a user selects some value. Now, we need to modify the existing templates and methods to allow the user to input the data into the form and see the results. We need to modify two files. The first one is again the action.class.php file of the menu module:

```
  /**
   * Executes index action
   * @param sfRequest $request A request object
   */
  public function executeIndex(sfWebRequest $request)
  {
    $this->form = new MilkshakeSearchForm();

    //Get all out all of the shakes
    $this->milkshakeObj = MilkShakePeer::getAllShakes
                          ($request->getParameter('page'),
                           sfConfig::get('mod_menu_total_menu_items'));

    //Forward to 404 if no results
    $this->forward404If($this->milkshakeObj->getNbResults() < 1,
                        'No Results in the Database');

    return sfView::SUCCESS;
  }
```

The second is the indexSuccess.php template file:

```
<?php use_javascript ('/js/jquery-1.3.2.min.js'); ?>
<?php use_javascript
              ('/sfFormExtraPlugin/js/jquery.autocompleter.js') ?>
<?php use_stylesheet
              ('/sfFormExtraPlugin/css/jquery.autocompleter.css') ?>

<form action="<?php echo url_for('menu/milkshake') ?>" method="POST">
<div style="text-align: center;">
```

```php
    <?php echo $form['url_slug']; ?>
    <input type="submit" value="Search" />
</div>
</form>

<?php $i=0 ?>

<?php foreach($milkshakeObj->getResults() as $milkshake): ?>
```

In this code, you can see an example of the use_javascript() and
use_stylesheet() functions. These functions can also be used instead of
configuring everything in the view.yml file. We are adding a form below
these functions. Please note that the form is redirecting to the menu/milkshake
page, and not to menu/index, because we are expecting to get an exact match for
the url_slug column.

The result of our coding is shown in the following screenshot:

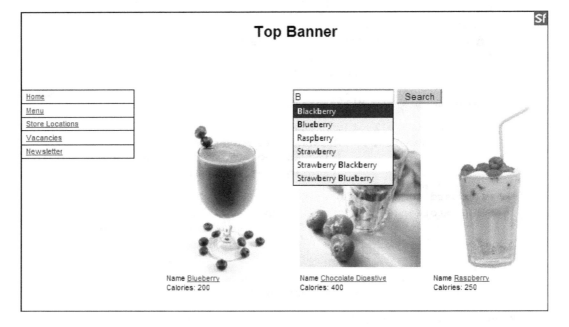

Other JavaScript helpers

Symfony also provides other JavaScript helpers, gathered together in the helper package JavascriptBaseHelper. These helpers are useful while working on code that is not based on forms. Here is a list of useful helpers:

Helper	Description
link_to_function()	Adds an onclick event that will trigger a function
button_to_function()	Same as above, but is applied to a button
array_or_string_for_JavaScript()	Converts a PHP array to a JavaScript one

Summary

In this chapter, we have learned how to handle more complicated M-N database relations, and how to add an autocomplete feature with little AJAX help. This knowledge will allow us to make better and more useful admin areas, and to create pages that can be used and managed easily. It is worth remembering that modern JavaScript libraries allow us to create professional effects very easily, and Symfony often makes this task even simpler. Creating M-N relations is very quick and easy, and can also save a lot of time that we would have to spend on coding and testing our own solutions. A very flexible admin generator along with a form handling system is one of the main advantages of Symfony.

7
Internationalizing our Global Positions

So far our milkshake web site is set up for English-speaking people. However, what happens when we want to open shops in other locations such as France where not everyone speaks English? In this chapter, we will address this problem by introducing internationalization and localization to parts of our application.

In this chapter, you will learn how to:

- Automatically set a user's preferred culture
- Allow a user to change his or her culture and language
- Use XLIFF dictionary files to translate template text
- Set up tables in the database to allow for several languages
- Understand about internationalization and localization

Internationalization and localization

Internationalizing and localizing a web site means that the site has another translation or several other translations. Not only is the text translated, but other forms of data such as dates, times, and currencies are transformed to match the locale.

This sounds great. But what happens if the user is a French Canadian, or an English Australian? For the former, this would mean that the language would have a French translation, but the date and currency would have to be Canadian. This is solved by a mixture of two standards.

1. Language code standards. (ISO 639-1) (`http://en.wikipedia.org/wiki/List_of_ISO_639-1_codes`)

2. Country code standards. (ISO 3166-1) (`http://en.wikipedia.org/wiki/ISO_3166-1`)

These standards are quite simple. Each language is represented as two characters in lowercase and each country is represented as two characters in uppercase. For example, the spoken language in the United Kingdom is English, which is represented as `en`; and the country is represented as `GB`. Therefore, if we combine the two, we get `en_GB`.

 Internationalization and localization are referred to as I18N and L10N, because Internationalization starts with an I, then is preceded by 18 characters followed by an N. The same logic is also applied to localization.

With this understanding, we are going to add I18n and L10n to the vacancies page so that a user can browse for jobs in his or her preferred locale and language, if it's available.

Refactoring the schema

The first thing that we need to do is adjust the `vacancies` table by splitting it into two tables that have a one-to-many relationship. The main table (`vacancies`) will contain only data that doesn't need translating, and the linking table (`vacancies_i18n`) will hold only translated content. Therefore, we can have many translations for each vacancy in the database.

Open up our project `schema.xml` file in the `config/` folder and find the `vacancies` table. Now replace its content with the following:

```
<table name="vacancies" idMethod="native" phpName="Vacancy"
    isI18N="true" i18nTable="vacancies_i18n" >
  <column name="id" type="INTEGER" required="true"
        autoIncrement="true" primaryKey="true"/>
  <column name="locations_id" type="INTEGER" required="true" />
    <foreign-key foreignTable="store_locations" onDelete="RESTRICT">
      <reference local="locations_id" foreign="id" />
    </foreign-key>
```

```
    <column name="closing_date" type="TIMESTAMP" required="true" />
</table>

<table name="vacancies_i18n" idMethod="native" phpName="VacancyI18n">
  <column name="id" type="INTEGER" required="true"
          primaryKey="true"/>
    <foreign-key foreignTable="vacancies" onDelete="CASCADE">
      <reference local="id" foreign="id" />
    </foreign-key>

  <column name="culture" type="VARCHAR" size="7" required="true"
          isCulture="true" primaryKey="true"   />

  <column name="position" type="VARCHAR" size="30" required="true" />
  <column name="position_description" type="VARCHAR" size="100"
          required="true" />
</table>
```

Looking at the schema, we can see that we have:

1. Created an additional table called vacancies_i18n.

 It is important that the table name matches the vacancies table with _i18n appended to it.

2. Removed the position and position_description columns from the vacancies table and added them into the vacancies_i18n table.

3. Added a foreign key column called id to the vacancies_i18n, which references the vacancies table's id column.

4. Created a culture column in the vacancies_i18n table, making sure that the isCulture attribute is set to true.

5. Added the isI18N and i18nTable attributes to the vacancies table.

The attributes, culture, and foreign key columns are very important in the schema because they are the enhancements to Propel. As they are enhancements, it means that Symfony and Propel are going to do the work for us, aiding us in not having to refactor much code.

 There is a shorthand way of producing the above structure which is documented on the Symfony site. However, the example schema is done in the YAML and not in the XML format. So, do expect problems if you wish to apply the shorthand method to your XML schema.

Rebuilding with test data

Before we do any coding, we ideally need to populate the database with additional test data so that we can test our page. Open up the `fixtures.yml` file in the `data/fixtures/` folder. At the bottom of the file, add the following:

```
Vacancy:
  va1:
    locations_id: 11
    closing_date: 2008-09-09
VacancyI18n:
  v1:
    id: va1
    position: Bonzza Shaker
    position_description: |
      Calling all shaker dudes/dudettes to Milkshake. Must shake shakes
and work the till
    culture: en_AU
  v2:
    id: va1
    position: Milkshaker
    position_description: |
      Calling all shakers to Milkshake. Must shake shakes and work the
till
    culture: en_GB
  v3:
    id: va1
    position: Un Milkshaker
    position_description: |
      Appeler tous les dispositifs trembleurs au milkshake. Doit
secouer des secousses et travailler jusqu'Ã
    culture: fr_FR
```

Let's recap over the `fixtures.yml` file. In it, there is an entry that will be inserted into the `vacancies` table. Once that is inserted, the `vacanies_i18n` table is populated with three entries representing three different translations. The relationship is also completed by using the `va1` subkey, which references the `id` vacancies.

Now that we have the schema and test data in place, let's re-build our models, insert the test data, and clear the cache.

```
$/home/timmy/workspace/milkshake>symfony propel:build-all-load --no
                              -confirmation && symfony cc
```

Just like all the other generated models, we have generated another five new models in the `lib/model` folder relating to the `vacancies_i18n` table. The base classes for the existing vacancies models were also updated to reflect the i18N additions.

When we modified the schema, I mentioned that the table naming convention, columns, and attributes were extremely important because they were enhancements. Now we can see how.

Most queries in our models are executed with the `doSelect()` function. This retrieves the results related to criteria. Of course, this would also use the same method for the `vacancies`, `vacancies_i18n`, and `location` tables. But when using i18n, a new method `doSelectWithI18n()` is created for us. This method does not only create the regular objects, but also transparently creates the related i18n objects.

In your `lib/model/` folder, let's open the `VacancyPeer.php` file and create a `getVacancies()` method:

```
public static function getVacancies($culture)
{
    return self::doSelectWithI18n(new Criteria, $culture);
}
```

Our web site is going to have a few different translations. Therefore, the function needs a `culture` to be passed into it.

Setting and getting the culture and language

The `sfUser` class provides both getter and setter methods for retrieving and setting a user's culture. This means that we can modify the culture for the user if we need to. We might do this if, for example, we had another translation and the user selected it.

To retrieve the culture, you would use the `sfUser` objects' `getCulture()` method:

```
$userCulture = $this->getUser()->getCulture();
```

To set the culture, use the `sfUser` objects' `setCulture()` method:

```
$this->getUser()->setCulture('en_AU');
```

As part of a request, your web browser includes the HTTP header `Accept-Language`. This tells the server what your preferred language is set to. For example, the `Accept-Language` header in my browser is:

```
Accept-Language en-au,en-gb;q=0.7,en;q=0.3
```

But a French user's browser might contain this:

```
Accept-Language fr;q=1.0,en;q=0.5
```

The header not only denotes the preferred language, but also the priority. The French user will obviously prefer French followed by English.

Preferred culture and language

The users' web browser contains both the culture and language, which means that if the user's preferred language is one that you provide, you could server them these pages instead.

We can access the users' languages through the request object:

```
$userLanguage = $this->getRequest()->getLanguages();
```

Using the getLanguages() method, an array of the languages will be returned.

The users' preferred culture can be accessed through the request objects' getPreferredCulture() method. You can also pass in the preferred language based on their settings. For example:

```
$culture = $request->getPreferredCulture(array('en', 'fr'))
```

The action

Now let's add the application logic to retrieve the vacancies based on the users' culture. We modified the model to allow us to pass in the culture; we also need to refactor the action. Open up the vacancies action class in apps/frontend/modules/vacancies/actions/actions.class.php and amend the index action:

```
    public function executeIndex()
    {

        $this->vacanciesArray = VacancyPeer::getVacancies($this->
                                         getUser()->getCulture());

        if(count($this->vacanciesArray) < 1)
        {
            return 'NoVacancies';
        }
        else
        {
```

```
        return sfView::SUCCESS;
    }

}
```

We have passed in the `culture` to our model using the user object. The logic also takes into account that there might not be any vacancies. This time we are going to create a template for this rather than setting a flash variable.

Let's create it now while we are on the subject of handling the no-vacancies pages. Create a new template in `apps/frontend/modules/vacancies/templates/indexNoVacancies.php`. The following is a simple template:

```
<h1>No Vacancies at present</h1>
```

(I did say it was simple!)

Adding culture to the routing

When creating several pages that contain translated versions of text, you need to allow each translation to have its own URL, which contains a `culture` parameter. For example, to access the French version of the vacancies page, the URL would be:

```
http://milkshake/fr_FR/vacancies
```

Therefore, we have to amend the current routing rule for the vacancy page. Open the `apps/frontend/config/routing.yml` file. Let's change the vacancies rule to automatically add the culture parameter for us and to also add a requirement that one of our cultures must be passed in.

```
vacancies
  url:    /:sf_culture/vacancies
  param: { module: vacancies, action: index }
  requirements:
    {sf_culture: (?:en_AU|en_GB|fr_FR)}
```

I have added the special `/:sf_culture` parameter to the URL and set the requirements for `sf_culture` to only allow the available cultures that our site supports. Before testing, make sure you clear the cache with this command:

```
>symfony cc
```

With everything in place, you can go ahead and view all three translated pages by checking these URLs:

`http://milkshake/frontend_dev.php/en_AU/vacancies`

`http://milkshake/frontend_dev.php/en_GB/vacancies`

`http://milkshake/frontend_dev.php/fr_FR/vacancies`

If you play around with the site, you will notice that the every time you select the **Vacancies** link, the culture in the URL is set to the one that you selected. This is because the user object is also updated with the new culture. Also, because the routing rule contains requirements, any variation in culture will result in a 404 error page.

Localizing the template

As you can see, clever handling of i18n means that we do not need to touch the template. But now we have a problem: Although the dynamic text is translated, the static template text is not and is displayed in English. Also, other cultures have different formatting for other types of information such as the date, time, and currency.

To address this problem, Symfony comes with template helpers to aid us with localization of the templates.

Continuing our work on the vacancies page, one field that we can localize is the close date field. There are three types of helper groups—Date, `Number`, and `I18N`—and none of them are enabled by default. So let's set the culture on the date field. First, we must declare at the top of the template that we want to use the `Date` helper. Therefore, in our `apps/frontend/modules/vacanies/templates/indexSuccess.php` template, add the following to the first line:

```
<?php use_helper('Date') ?>
```

Now that the `Date` helper is enabled, we can go ahead and use it. Change the following line

```
<?php echo $vacancy?>getClosingDate('d/m/Y') ?>
```

to:

```
<?php echo format_date($vacancy->getClosingDate()) ?>
```

Translating interface text

Although the data that is stored in the database has three translations, we still need to address the static text on the template. Although Symfony provides several options, we will stick to the default, which is **XLIFF (XML Localization Interchange File Format)**.

XLIFF is an XML-based format for localization that is partly integrated into the `I18N` helper. Any text on the template that needs to be translated should be passed into the `__()` function. The text is then looked up in a dictionary file. If a match is found, the translated version is sent back.

The dictionary files are in an XML format and should be named `messages.[language].xml` and stored in either the `application i18n/` folder or the `module i18n/` folder, depending on whether or not they're global.

Of course, the dictionary files can be structured by name. I have chosen to use the default name, `messages`, as a part of the filename. You can, however, prepend something a little more meaningful rather than `message`, as long as you pass that to the helper.

Configuring i18n for the templates

By default, the i18n support in Symfony is turned off. Therefore, we have to turn it on. Open up the frontend application setting's file in `apps/frontend/config`, so that we can turn on i18n. There are three modifications that we have to make. Add the following to the end of the settings, just underneath the `enabled_modules` key that we created earlier:

1.

. . .

```
enabled_modules:        [default,alSignup]

  i18n:                 on
```

2.
```
  standard_helpers:     [Partial, Cache, Form, I18N]
```
3.
```
  default_culture:      en_GB
```

Dictionary files

Dictionary files are in an XML format and provide a lookup based on the text from the template that is passed into the __() helper. Each translation contains its own dictionary file that resides in the apps/frontend/i18n/{culture} folder and is named accordingly. For example, the translation dictionary file for fr_FR would reside in apps/frontend/i18n/fr/messages.xml and would look like the following:

```
<?xml version="1.0" encoding="UTF-8"?>
<!DOCTYPE xliff PUBLIC "-//XLIFF//DTD XLIFF//EN"
                    "http://www.oasis-open.org/committees/
                            xliff/documents/xliff.dtd">
<xliff version="1.0">
  <file source-language="EN" target-language="fr"
        datatype="plaintext" original="messages"
        date="2009-05-18T20:59:37Z" product-name="messages">
    <header/>
    <body>
      <trans-unit id="1">
        <source>For further information please contact H.R at our main
                                          branch.</source>

        <target>Veuillez pour de plus amples informations entrent en
                contact avec H.R Ã  notre branche principale.</target>
      </trans-unit>
      <trans-unit id="2">
        <source>Closing Date</source>
        <target>Date limite</target>
      </trans-unit>
        <trans-unit id="3">
        <source>Wanted in</source>
        <target>Voulu dedans</target>
      </trans-unit>
        <trans-unit id="4">
        <source>Current vacanies</source>
        <target>Vacanies courants</target>
      </trans-unit>
    </body>
  </file>
</xliff>
```

The file is very straightforward. Looking at the bold entry:

- Each text translation is in a `<trans-unit>` tag and contains a unique ID.

  Inside the `<source>` tag is the text that is located on the template. It's passed to the `__()` helper.

  In our example our template will contain the following:

  ```php
  <?php echo __('For further information please contact H.R at our main branch.</source>') ?>
  ```

- This is the text that is searched for.

- Once a match has been found in the `<source>` tag, the text in the `<target>` tag is then returned.

Although these files look a little tedious to do, Symfony does provide a task that will create all this for us. We will use it in the next section.

 You can find out more about the XML structure at http://docs.oasis-open.org/xliff/v1.2/os/xliff-core.html#source-language.

Translating the interface

In order to bring this all together, we are going to create the links that allow a user to select one of the three languages. Secondly, we are going to pass all the static template text into the `i18N` helper.

Adding the culture links

The first part is straightforward and requires us to make a basic set of links for subnavigation style. In the `indexSuccess.php` template located in the `app/frontend/modules/vacancies/templates` folder, add the following code in bold:

```php
<?php use_helper('Date') ?>
<div style="width: 100px; float:right">
<?php echo link_to(image_tag('/images/flags/en_GB.png'),
                   '@vacancies?sf_culture=en_GB') ?> 
<?php echo link_to(image_tag('/images/flags/en_AU.png'),
                   '@vacancies?sf_culture=en_AU') ?> 
<?php echo link_to(image_tag('/images/flags/fr_FR.png'),
                   '@vacancies?sf_culture=fr_FR') ?>
</div>
```

We have added three links, one for each culture. Unlike the main navigation, we have small images representing the links. Therefore, rather that inserting text as the link name, we use the `image_tag()` helper and pass in the URL to the image. Because we have already set up the vacancies routing to insert the culture, we can also use the routing tag of `@vacancies` to reference this route.

Translating the static text

Let's start by translating the word **Postion:** on the template. Find the word `Position:`

```
<strong>Position: </strong> <?php echo $vacancy->getPosition(); ?>
```

Now change it to the following:

```
<strong><?php echo __('Position:') ?></strong>
<?php echo $vacancy->getPosition(); ?>
```

We have to take the text and pass it into the `i18N` helper. Now it's time to create the dictionary files for this. We need three files in total—Australian, British, and French.

As mentioned earlier, Symfony will generate these files for us. In the terminal, enter:

>symfony i18n:extract frontend fr –auto-save --auto-delete

You will see the following output in the terminal:

```
timmy@timmys-laptop:~/workspace/milkshake$ symfony i18n:extract frontend fr --auto-save
>> i18n       extracting i18n strings for the "frontend" application
>> i18n       found "1" new i18n strings
>> i18n       found "0" old i18n strings
>> i18n       saving new i18n strings
```

We have passed in four variables to the i18N task. They are:

1. `frontend`: Name of the applications
2. `fr`: The culture we want the translation for
3. `--auto-save`: Saves all new strings to our catalogue
4. `--auto-delete`: Deletes all strings that have been removed from the template

The output informs us that it is searching our frontend application and has found one string that needs to be translated. Also, there are no strings to be removed. As we have only asked for the `Position` text to be translated on the vacancies template, this adds up.

If you look inside the `apps/frontend/i18N` folder, you will find that a new folder has been created for us — `fr`. The folder name represents the culture. Inside this folder, the `messages.xml` dictionary file resides.

Let's have a quick look at the `messages.xml` file:

```
<?xml version="1.0" encoding="UTF-8"?>
<!DOCTYPE xliff PUBLIC "-//XLIFF//DTD XLIFF//EN"
                       "http://www.oasis-open.org/committees/
                                    xliff/documents/xliff.dtd">
<xliff version="1.0">
  <file source-language="EN" target-language="fr"
        datatype="plaintext" original="messages"
        date="2009-05-18T20:59:37Z" product-name="messages">
    <header/>
    <body>
      <trans-unit id="1">
        <source>Title:</source>
        <target/>
      </trans-unit>
    </body>
  </file>
</xliff>
```

Although the file has been created for use, we will have to manually add the French translation for `Title:` inside the `target` tag. Change `<target />` to:

```
<target>Title</target>
```

Now that you have seen how easy it is, let's translate the rest of the template text. Below is the final template, in which I have placed the amends in bold:

```
<?php use_helper('Date') ?>
<div style="width: 100px; float:right">
<?php echo link_to(image_tag('/images/flags/en_GB.png'),
                   '@vacancies') ?> 
<?php echo link_to(image_tag('/images/flags/en_AU.png'),
                   '@vacancies') ?> 
<?php echo link_to(image_tag('/images/flags/fr_FR.png'),
                   '@vacancies') ?>
</div>
<h3 style="margin-top:0; padding-top:0">Current Vacancies</h3>
<?php foreach($vacanciesArray as $vacancy): ?>
<div style="margin-bottom: 10px;">
  <strong><?php echo __('Position') ?></strong>
   <?php echo $vacancy->getPosition(); ?><br />
  <strong><?php echo __('Job Description:') ?></strong>
```

```php
        <?php echo $vacancy->getPositionDescription(); ?><br /><br />
    <strong><?php echo __('Closing date:') ?></strong>
        <?php echo format_date($vacancy->getClosingDate()) ?><br />
</div>
<br />
<?php __('For further information please contact H.R at our
                                        main branch.') ?>

<?php endforeach ?>
```

With the template now complete, let's re-run the task on the command line:

```
>symfony i18n:extract frontend fr –auto-save --auto-delete
```

After the task is finished, it will report that three other strings for translation were found:

```
timmy@timmys-laptop:~/workspace/milkshake$ symfony i18n:extract frontend fr --auto-save --auto-delete
>> i18n     extracting i18n strings for the "frontend" application
>> i18n     found "3" new i18n strings
>> i18n     found "0" old i18n strings
>> i18n     saving new i18n strings
>> i18n     deleting old i18n strings
```

The following is the final French dictionary file created for us in apps/frontend/i18N/fr/messages.xml and completed with translation:

```xml
<?xml version="1.0" encoding="UTF-8"?>
<!DOCTYPE xliff PUBLIC "-//XLIFF//DTD XLIFF//EN"
                    "http://www.oasis-open.org/committees/
                                    xliff/documents/xliff.dtd">
<xliff version="1.0">
  <file source-language="EN" target-language="fr"
        datatype="plaintext" original="messages"
        date="2009-05-18T23:54:19Z" product-name="messages">
    <header/>
    <body>
      <trans-unit id="1">
        <source>Position:</source>
        <target>Position:</target>
      </trans-unit>
      <trans-unit id="2">
        <source>Job Description:</source>
        <target>Description des fonctions:</target>
      </trans-unit>
      <trans-unit id="3">
        <source>Closing date:</source>
        <target>Date limite:</target>
      </trans-unit>
```

```
    <trans-unit id="4">
        <source>For further information please contact H.R at our main
branch.</source>
        <target>Veuillez pour de plus amples informations entrent en
                contact avec H.R à notre branche principale.</target>
    </trans-unit>
  </body>
 </file>
</xliff>
```

Repeating the earlier steps, go ahead and create the other two translations:

```
>symfony i18n:extract frontend en_GB –auto-save –auto-delete
>symfony i18n:extract frontend en_AU –auto-save --auto-delete
```

We still need to create a en_GB version because if we viewed the page in **French** and then wanted the to view the en_GB version, there would be no dictionary file to translate it back.

Summary

Translating your site using Symfony is painlessly simple. Although we have only added the functionality to one page, adding it to the whole site is not too much of a problem. One point to remember before you even begin to build is to ask the question: 'Will this site require i18n?' This question will have implications on your database later on.

Through this chapter we familiarized ourselves both with the users' culture and languages, and saw how Symfony makes translation of dynamic text simple. Another key feature is the Symfony task that creates the XLIFF dictionary files for us.

8
Extending Symfony

So far we have seen one way to extend the Symfony framework, that is, by downloading and installing third-party plugins that have aided us by adding whole components without the need to recode. Also, we have added email functionality by using the Swift Mailer, which is a third-party library. In this chapter, we are going to extend this further by bridging another framework to Symfony.

In this chapter you will learn how to:

- Integrate components from other frameworks into Symfony
- Create and extend core framework classes

Bridging to other frameworks

There are many standalone components and frameworks that incorporate vast units of functionality, and using them in your project will save you time. But using Symfony requires you to develop in a certain way. Of course, it makes no sense in re-coding the components just to make them fit in with Symfony. Therefore, the Symfony framework provides autoloading, which allows you to plug in and play.

Bridging with eZ Components

eZ Components is a collection of PHP components that can be easily added to any project to provide a vast unit of functionality.

To demonstrate the simplicity of using other libraries such as eZ Components, we are going to use the eZ graph component. This will be used to display a pie chart of the selected milkshake flavors.

To start with, we must download eZ Components from their web site at `http://ezcomponents.org/download`. Once you have downloaded the libraries, create a new folder called `ezcomponents` within the `lib/vendor` directory. Once the folder is created, extract and copy the `autoload`, `base`, and `graph` folders of eZ Components into the new `ezcomponents` folder that you just created. The directory structure should resemble the following:

```
lib/vendor/ezcomponents/
                        /autoload
                        /base
                        /graph
```

Configuring the component with Symfony

Due to the vast amount of files that come with eZ Components, ideally we would like Symfony to autoload these for us. To do this, we are first going to set the location of eZ Components and then extend Symfony's autoloading to load these files.

In our frontend configuration file (`apps/frontend/congif/app.yml`), add the location of eZ Components as follows:

```
all:
  ez_lib_dir:   <?php echo sfConfig::get('sf_root_dir') ?>/lib/vendor/
ezcomponents
```

Next, we have to extend Syfmony's autoloading. As this is only needed for our frontend application, we need to open the application's configuration class, located at `apps/frontend/config/frontendConfiguration.class.php`, and insert the following:

```php
<?php

class frontendConfiguration extends sfApplicationConfiguration
{
  public function configure()
  {
  }

  public function initialize()
  {
    //eZ Components
    if ($sf_ez_lib_dir = sfConfig::get('app_ez_lib_dir'))
    {
      set_include_path($sf_ez_lib_dir.PATH_SEPARATOR.get_include_
                                                     path());

      require_once($sf_ez_lib_dir.'/Base/src/base.php');
```

```
        spl_autoload_register(array('ezcBase', 'autoload'));
    }
  }
}
```

By using the `spl_autoload_register()` function of PHP, we pass the name of the base class of eZ Components. Thus, eZ Components is now autoloaded for us.

Using the component

We will create a new module called `best` to handle the functionality of retrieving the data and displaying the graph. I have created my module and named it `best` using this command:

`$/home/timmy/workspace/milkshake>symfony  generate:module frontend best`

First, we need to create the business logic that retrieves the results from the database for use. Open the `lib/model/MilkShakePeer.php` file and create the following new function:

```
public static function getBestMilkshakes()
{
    $milkshakeResults =  DbFinder::from('Milkshake')->find();

    return $milkshakeResults;
}
```

With the business logic in place, we can start working on the application logic in the action class. Opening the action class in the `best` module from `apps/frontend/modules/best/actions/actions.class.php`, simply replace the default index action with the following:

```
public function executeIndex()
{
    //Get the results
    $milkshakeArray = MilkShakePeer::getAllMilkshakes();

    foreach($milkshakeArray as $key => $val)
    {
        $viewArray[$val->getMilkShake()->getName()] =
                       $val->getMilkShake()->getViews();
    }
    $graph = new ezcGraphPieChart();
    $graph->title = 'Favourite Flavours';
```

```
$graph->title->maxHeight = 0.1;
$graph->legend = false;
$graph->data['Access statistics'] = new
                           ezcGraphArrayDataSet($viewArray);

 $graph->driver = new ezcGraphGdDriver();
$graph->options->font = '/usr/share/fonts/truetype
                              /msttcorefonts/arial.ttf';
$graph->driver->options->supersampling = 1;
$graph->driver->options->jpegQuality = 100;
$graph->driver->options->imageFormat = IMG_JPEG;

//render image
$graph->render(560, 500, 'images/charts/pie_chart.jpg' );
return sfView::SUCCESS;
}
```

We start by retrieving all of the milkshakes in the database, and then add the milkshake names and views to an associative array. This array will be passed into the eZ graph component.

The code in bold demonstrates the magic of the `sfEzComponentsBridge` by allowing us to use the eZ graphs component as we would with any other class, without having to use the `php include()` function.

I have used some of the custom methods that can be found on the components' documentation page to lay out the pie chart. As soon as the page is accessed, the graphing component will create the graph and store it on the file system. Of course, I have chosen the easy approach to use in our milkshake site. But you can take the process further by possibly generating the pie graph on-the-fly.

Finally, open the template from `apps/frontend/modules/best/templates/indexSuccess.php`, and add the following tag. This will display the graph on the page.

```
<?php echo image_tag('/images/charts/pie_chart.jpg') ?>
```

Before testing the new module, we have to complete four remaining tasks:

- Define the routing rules into our application
- Create the directory where we will save the graph
- Update the site navigation to allow users to navigate to the page
- Clear the cache

Open the frontend application's routing file, located at `apps/frontend/config/`
`routing.yml`, and add the following rule to direct all the requests of `/best` to our
new module and action:

```
best:
  url: /best
  param: { module: best, action: index}
```

I have defined the location of where the eZ graph component will store the
graphics — `images/charts/`. So, create the folder and set the permissions as follows
to allow the web server to write to the directory:

```
>mkdir images/charts; chmod 777 images/charts
```

Finally, add a link to the navigation so that the user can access the results page:

```
<?php echo link_to('Best Flavours', '@best') ?>
```

After all the steps are complete, clear the cache. Now select at least one milkshake
from the menu before viewing the best milkshakes page. From the following graph
you can see that I have viewed three milkshakes from the menu:

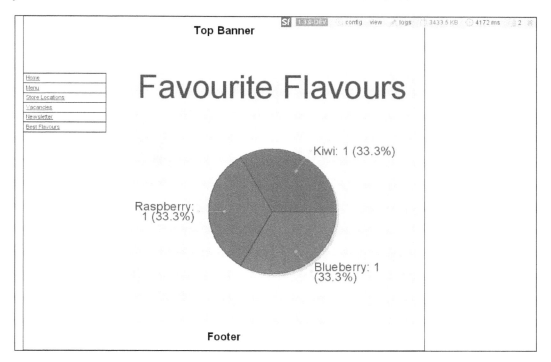

Bridging with the Zend Framework

The Zend Framework is bridged in exactly the same manner as the eZ Components are bridged into Symfony. eZ Components has a good library of components. This also goes for the Zend Framework that has some good features to offer as well. Some of the most noted components in the Zend Framework are:

- The Zend_Search_Lucene that provides text searching and ranking
- The Zend_Rest web services
- The Zend_Service that provides support to some of the popular web services

Extending the core classes with your own

In object-orientated programming, the factory pattern is a way of having one class that is responsible for creating objects. That means the pattern's sole purpose is the responsibility for the creation of objects. In Symfony, it is used to create all of the core objects of the framework.

In some instances, you might need to extend one of the core classes, or perhaps replace it with your own. Symfony makes this very simple as the factory settings are conveniently located in the application's config/ folder. When we look at the main factory settings for our frontend application in the factories.yml file, located at apps/frontend/config/factories.yml, we see this:

```
prod:
  logger:
    class:    sfNoLogger
    param:
      level:    err
      loggers: ~

cli:
  controller:
    class: sfConsoleController
  request:
    class: sfConsoleRequest
  response:
    class: sfConsoleResponse

test:
  storage:
    class: sfSessionTestStorage
    param:
      session_path: %SF_TEST_CACHE_DIR%/sessions
```

```
response:
  class: sfWebResponse
  param:
    send_http_headers: false
all:
  routing:
    class: sfPatternRouting
    param:
      generate_shortest_url:              true
      extra_parameters_as_query_string:   true
```

Looking at the controller, for example, the factory instantiates the
sfFrontWebController—the main entry point into the application. Of course,
it is easy to modify the sfFrontWebController if needed. It's as simple as
creating your own class that extends the sfFrontWebController, and
updating the factories.yml file with the name of your new class.

For example, you could create myWebController that extends
sfFrontWebController and then extend it for your needs. Then in the
factories.yml file, you would replace sfFrontWebController with
myWebController, and uncomment. Now you will have extended one of
Symfony's core classes.

In the closing chapters, we will see this in action when we modify the factories
configuration by changing the session and the view cache.

Multiple inheritance

One feature that PHP lacks is multiple inheritance. That means a class can only
extend one parent and not several classes. This presents the developers with a
limitation on how they design their classes. To address this limitation, there is a
known pattern called a **mixin**. A mixin is like a partial class that can be 'mixed in' to
another class in order to supply extended functionality. Since these classes provide
extra functionality, they can be reused.

To aid users with mixins, Symfony has a sfMixer class. The class that requires the
mixin must extend a parent, and then declare and register the extensions using the
sfMixer class.

 Symfony only provides a class for mixin, most of the complex
sites don't really require use of mixins.

Summary

Symfony is a loosely coupled framework, which means that a lot of functionality that has been implemented in other classes and frameworks can be integrated with it. We have seen throughout the book how plugins can save a great deal of time. In this chapter, we extended this by introducing components and adding the eZ graph component. If Symfony does need that extra something for use in your own applications, it can easily be extended to meet your needs.

In addition to using other components, we have also seen how we can extend the core classes of Symfony. This allows us to introduce our own logic.

Optimizing for Performance

9

We now have a site that runs relatively fast. However, just because the site is fast doesn't mean we should leave it at that. There are times when fast is not fast enough. This chapter is all about optimizing our site by introducing compression and caching. We will start by looking at and using Symfony's caching framework before pushing Symfony's cache out to a caching server.

By the end of this chapter, you will know how to:

- Use Symfony's caching framework
- Optimize database calls through Propel by creating your own SQL calls and skipping the hydration process
- Configure Symfony to help client-side caching
- Configure Symfony to use `memcached`

HTTP compression

Every time a user makes a request, the request goes through Symfony's execution chain, queries the database (if needed), and then renders the view. This processing creates an overhead and depending on several factors, can eventually slow a site down. There are numerous methods that can be deployed in order to speed up the processing, by efficiently utilizing other resources.

The first step in speeding up our application is the delivery of the page content to the user's browser. When a user makes a request to the web server, a part of the request consists of various headers. One of the headers is the 'Accept-Encoding' header, which is usually set to Gzip or Deflate. This tells the server that the browser can accept content that is either compressed as Gzip or Deflate.

To enable compression, we have to turn it *on* in the settings. Open the `settings.yml` file, and then look for the `compressed` parameter key halfway down. Uncomment the parameter key and change its value from *off* to *on*.

You can find the `settings.yml` file at `apps/frontend/config/settings.yml`:

```
compressed:                on
```

After making the change to the `settings.yml` file, you must also clear the cache using this:

```
$/home/timmy/workspace/milkshake>symfony cc
```

Using the Firebug extension in Firefox, you will see the difference in page weight. For example, I am going to view the menu page. I have taken a screenshot of the headers from Firebug before turning the compression on. As you can see in the following screenshot, the total page size is **113 KB**.

After enabling the compression in the `settings.yml` file, the page size decreased from **113 KB** to **10 KB** as seen in the following screenshot:

If you compare the before and after views in Firebug, you will also notice a difference in both the returned headers and, of course, the page size. Looking at the above headers, notice the two extra response headers:

Content-Encoding: gzip

Vary: Accept Encoding

As you can see, **Content-Encoding** specifies that the content is encoded as **gzip**. Although the page is now around 11% of its original size, the server must do a little more processing to compress the final content. Also, this figure is only the size of the overall page weight.

In this chapter we will be creating and editing YAML files that contain settings for cache.

 It is important that you clear the cache every time you make any changes, and don't forget to use spaces instead of tabs when editing any of the YAML files.

Caching

As seen in the previous section, using HTTP compression is a step in the right direction. But we should really look at how to speed up Symfony before the final content is compressed and delivered. The solution to this is the use of caching. To limit the amount of processing required, Symfony offers a caching framework. Basically, it stores chunks of your code as native PHP in a temporary file. But it is not just the amount of processing that is saved through the framework. Result sets fetched from the database too can be cached, which means less connections to the database server and less processing by the database server too. By default, these temporary cache files are stored in the `cache/` folder, which we touched upon while creating the back office.

Essentially, Symfony will first check the `cache` directory before processing the configuration. If caching is enabled, there is no need to execute the action that ultimately speeds up the response and/or the layout. However, this will depend on what caching options you have specified.

Symfony offers several caching features for your application, which are:

- An action
- An action with layout
- A partial
- A component
- A component slot
- A template fragment

Cache settings

There are two ways in which we can enable caching. The first way is to enable caching globally and disable it on a page-by-page basis where it is not needed. The second way is to leave the cache disabled globally and enable caching only on a page-by-page basis.

The first step in enabling the cache is to amend our application settings in the `settings.yml` file located at `apps/frontend/config/settings.yml`. Here, we want to enable caching within the `dev` environment for the time being:

```
dev:
  .settings:
    error_reporting:        <?PHP echo (E_ALL | E_STRICT)."\n" ?>
    web_debug:              on
    cache:                  on
    no_script_name:         off
    etag:                   off
```

Caching globally

Although we are going to use caching on a module basis, let's have a quick look at how we could do this globally. This option is really great if you have a small, and possibly static, web site or if the site content is not frequently updated.

Open `apps/frontend/conf/cache.yml`:

```
default:
  enabled: off
  with_layout: false
  lifetime: 86400
```

These three settings in the `cache.yml` file allow us to enable caching globally:

- `enabled`: This enables caching for the whole application.

- `with_layout`: Caching is set to cache the action, and not the overall template by default. There are some occasions where the whole template cannot be cached. But by enabling this, both the template and the layout will be cached.

- `lifetime`: The cache is set to delete itself 24 hours after the caching occurs. This can be altered too.

As we want to enable the caching on a page-by-page basis, we can leave the global caching set to off.

Caching page-by-page

As you probably have already guessed, we will need to create a configuration file in each module to enable caching page-by-page. Let's start with the locations page. In the location module, we need to create a `cache.yml` file inside the `config/` folder. This will hold the cache settings for our locations module. Therefore, create the `apps/frontend/modules/locations/config/cache.yml` file and add the following:

```
index:
  enabled: on
all:
  with_layout: false
```

Once this has been done, we need to clear the cache. Again, remember that when editing any of these files, you will need to do this:

$/home/timmy/workspace/milkshake>symfony cc

We have now enabled caching for the locations page.

Caching without the layout

Before we take a look at the results, let's look at the Symfony log before caching was enabled as this will show a comparison on how effective caching is. To view this, we are going to use the web debug toolbar. On the toolbar, click on the clock icon, which is the second icon from the right, or the time next to the icon.

A quick look at the web debug toolbar shows us three useful variables: the total processing time (in ms), total database calls, and (after clicking on the **logs** link) the calls along with their times. Before I enabled the caching, I can see on my screen that it took approximately **4293 ms** and there were two database calls. Also, there was considerable time spent on the **Action** and **Configuration**.

Now let's take a look at the results after enabling the caching and doing a few refreshes in the browser:

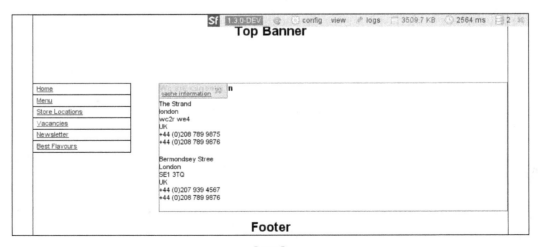

The previous screenshot shows the first request on the locations page after the caching was enabled. There are two main points here to note:

- The time has decreased largely.
- Our cached action contains a red box and a blue information box. This outlines what is cached, and also provides useful information about the cached segment. (You must click on the **cache information** link.)

The next request will come from cache. So just refreshing the page will display something similar to the following screenshot:

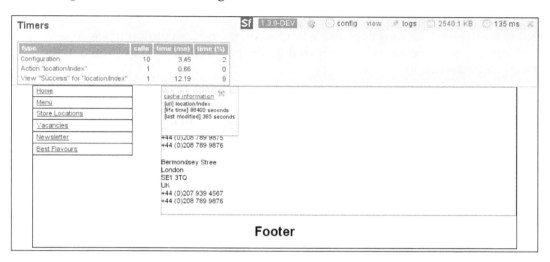

Now the **cache information** box is a pale yellow box, which signifies that this action template comes from the cache. Here are three other points to note:

- The time has decreased further to **135 ms**
- The time taken on the action has severely decreased
- There are no longer any calls to the database as now there is no database icon in the web debug toolbar

Caching with the layout

So far we have only cached the action template. As our site does not require any dynamic content, that is, a session based on the locations page, we can cache the layout too. When the template is cached, it is stored in the cache folder as an HTML file and returned with the response.

To enable this, we simply set the `with_layout` option to `true` in the `cache.yml` file that we set up earlier. The `cache.yml` file is located at `apps/frontend/modules/location/config/cache.yml`:

```
index:
  enabled: on
all:
  with_layout: true
```

Once you have done this, clear the cache:

```
$/home/timmy/workspace/milkshake>symfony cc
```

Now, revisit the locations page twice or click on the refresh button twice. You will first see the blue cache box followed by the pale yellow box, as shown in the following screenshot:

If we click on the clock icon or time link again, it will display this:

We have now cached both the action template and the layout. You can see this because the red layout box is wrapped around the entire page. Also, you can see again there are no database calls and the time has further decreased. If you look at the log, you will also see that both the action and the action template have been skipped.

Caching parts of a template

Caching fragments within a template has to be done within the templates itself. When caching fragments, the action is executed. But this, of course, does not save as much overheads as caching the action.

Dynamic cache

When you need to use dynamic cache, you have to use a filter that must be executed in the filter chain before `sfCacheFilter`. You would perhaps want to use dynamic cache, for example, a rating system. After a user has voted, he/she will always see the vote entered in the cached page, whereas everyone who hasn't voted would see the voting stars.

Cache storage

Till now we have used the default caching behavior, which is to save cache to the file system in the `cache` directory. However, we can change this through the `factories.yml`, which we looked at earlier, to store the cache in an alternative location if needed.

Looking at the cache settings in the `apps/frontend/config/factories.yml` file, we can see the default values that are commented out:

```
#  view_cache:
#    class: sfFileCache
#    param:
#      automaticCleaningFactor: 0
#      cacheDir:                %SF_TEMPLATE_CACHE_DIR%
#      lifetime:                86400
#      prefix:                  %SF_APP_DIR%/template
```

Here we could change the class to `sfSQLiteCache`, for example, which would allow us to use a SQLite database instead. At the end of the chapter, we will be taking a look at how to implement caching with `memcached`.

Caching dynamic pages

When a user updates a section through the backend, the frontend should be able to display those changes. Of course, if the frontend page is cached, these changes will not show. There are two approaches for this. The first is to set the cache time to a lower value. This will mean that the update will have to wait until the cache expires. This is great for smaller sites that do not need to be updated instantly. The second way is to delete the section of cache that holds the data. We can add the following code, and `save` the action to `/lib/forms/StoreLocationForm.class.php`:

```
public function configure()
{
}


public function save($con = null)
{
  // we are setting directory to to <env>/template/milkshake/all,
  // because we caching whole page layout (option with_layout = true,
  // not just module itself
  $frontend_cache_dir = sfConfig::get('sf_cache_dir').
    DIRECTORY_SEPARATOR.'frontend'.DIRECTORY_SEPARATOR.
    sfConfig::get('sf_environment').DIRECTORY_SEPARATOR.'template'.
    DIRECTORY_SEPARATOR.'milkshake'.DIRECTORY_SEPARATOR.'all';

  $cache = new sfFileCache(array(
    'cache_dir' => $frontend_cache_dir
  ));
  $cache->removePattern('location/index');

  return parent::save($con);
}
```

Looking at the database

Our web site connects to the database, executes a query, and then returns the result set. We can start looking at how we can improve its performance here. Some of the things that we can do are create custom queries and, possibly, replace the ORM layer.

Setting limits and columns in the criteria

Propel is very powerful when it comes to building a relatively complex SQL criteria. But the default criteria assumes that all columns are required if you do not explicitly specify them. To do this, you can use the addSelectColumn() method:

```
clearSelectColumns();
addSelectColumn(self::COLUMN_NAME);
```

Also, you can set a limit when you need only one result:

```
setLimit($limit);
```

For further documentation on the criteria class, refer to the Propel documentation at http://propel.phpdb.org/docs/api/1.3/runtime/propel-util/Criteria.html.

Creating your own SQL statements

As you have seen while using Propel, it is very simple to create a criteria and pass it to Propel, which then returns the results as objects. There are two situations when this can be overkill: when you have a very complicated query, or when you need a few smaller queries. The solution is to skip the hydration process and create your own query.

For example, if we wanted to create a custom query for locations, we would first amend the LocationPeer model by removing the DbFinder call and replacing it with Propel's PDO methods. Open the LocationsPeer.php file at lib/model/LocationPeer.php and make the following changes in it:

```
public static function getAllLocations()
{
  $con = Propel::getConnection();
  $stmt = $con->prepare("SELECT address1, address2, address3,
                         postcode, city, country, phone, fax
                         FROM locations ORDER BY City");
  $stmt->execute();

   return $stmt;
}
```

I have created the SQL query here and executed the statement using the Propel API.

The last thing we have to amend is the template located at apps/frontend/ modules/locations/templates/indexSuccess.php, as we are now passing a PDO object to it:

```
<h3 style="margin-top:0; padding-top:0">We are currently in</h3>
<?php while ($location = $locationsArray->fetchObject()): ?>
<div style="margin-bottom: 16px;">
   <?php echo $location->address1; ?><br />
   <?php echo ($location->address2 != "")? $location->address2.
                                        "<br />": ""; ?>
   <?php echo ($location->address3 != "")? $location->address3.
                                        "<br />": ""; ?>
   <?php echo $location->city; ?><br />
   <?php echo $location->postcode; ?><br />
   <?php echo $location->country; ?><br />
   <?php echo $location->phone; ?><br />
   <?php echo $location->fax; ?><br />
</div>
<?php endwhile; ?>
```

Just to show you the difference in terms of time, I ran the the query and looked at the database query times in the web debug toolbar. The results showed that preparing our own statement was slight faster at 0.16 ms, as opposed to 0.22 ms.

 For more information on Propel, please visit the Propel web site at http://propel.phpdb.org/trac/wiki/Users/ Documentation/1.3 and, of course, the PHP PDO pages at http://ww.php.net/pdo, as Propel 1.3 uses PDO.

Limit your queries

As mentioned above, limiting the amount of queries will save some response time. Creating your own queries, as shown in the previous section, is a good way of querying only for what you need. Two of the major downfalls for Propel are:

- It has a tendency to execute more queries than what is needed
- Developers end up creating more queries than needed because they are very easy to create

The only advice is to check the number of queries made, which is visible in the web debug toolbar.

You also should try to join tables if you want to use object relations. This is especially important in the backend area. You can add a `peer_method` under the list section in the `generator.yml` file:

```
list:
    peer_method: doSelectJoinAll
```

When you are creating a Propel object with Foreign-Key relations, a generator will automatically create a few methods such as:

- doSelectJoin<Model>
- doSelectJoinAllExcept<Model>
- doSelectJoinAll

Here `<Model>` means the related table and model.

Caching your queries

Just like all other elements, database queries can be cached as we have seen in the caching framework. At the end of the chapter, we will look at caching these with `memcached` and DbFinderPlugin.

ETags

An **entity tag** (**ETag**) is one of the HTTP headers that is returned to the browser. Its purpose is to inform the browser if the page has changed since it was last viewed. To enable this per environment, open the application's `settings.yml` file from `apps/frontend/config/settings.yml` and set it to `on`:

```
dev:
  .settings:
    error_reporting:       <?php echo (E_ALL | E_STRICT)."\n" ?>
    web_debug:             on
    cache:                 off
    no_script_name:        off
    etag:                  on
```

Less requests

As I mentioned, once a page is formed, your browser reads the HTML and then retrieves all the required resources. For example, most pages contain external links to stylesheets and JavaScript files. For each one that is encountered, the browser must make another request to the server, retrieve the resource, and then parse it. All this takes time, especially if you have large JavaScript files.

Decreasing the number of requests would mean that all of the style information and JavaScript should be included with the template.

Stylesheets

There are four ways to include styles. They are:

- Inline styles
- Using a partial that contains the styles
- Linking them in the header
- Setting them in the template's `view.yml` file

All unique styles should, of course, be written in the header between the `<style></style>` tags as this prevents the bloating of your stylesheet. Finally, remove the external stylesheet from the `view.yml` file and create a partial that contains the entire stylesheet for you. This approach keeps your templates tidy, but includes the styles.

JavaScripts

In Chapter 6, *Advanced Forms and Javascript*, we learned how to include JavaScript. However, although using a plugin may appear to be easier, I generally use the following guidelines:

1. Download your favorite JavaScript library in a packed form and add it to the main template when needed. (I do not recommend adding it to the main layout template if all the other templates do not require it). Place this at the bottom of your template.

2. Rather than using the Symfony helpers, write your own JavaScript.

3. When you are done with your own JavaScript, pack the JavaScript.

 To pack your JavaScript, you should use either a *packer* or *minifier* tool, one of which is **Dean Edwards' Packer** (`http://dean.edwards.name/packer/`).

Other tools to aid you

Symfony provides many features to not only aid in rapidly developing an application, but also in speeding up the response times as users access your site. Just like any other web framework, there are always other tools and tricks that are available to help you test your application and the server in which it resides. Therefore, the last section is dedicated to some of the most popular tools that I actually use to target bottlenecks in applications. This aids me into fixing them and making the application perform faster.

Firefox developer tools

Firefox has some very nice tools to help you optimize your web application. These are the four that I constantly find myself using:

- Yslow — https://addons.mozilla.org/en-US/firefox/addon/5369
- Firebug — https://addons.mozilla.org/en-US/firefox/addon/1843
- Firephp — https://addons.mozilla.org/en-US/firefox/addon/6149
- Web developer tools — https://addons.mozilla.org/en-US/firefox/addon/60

Install them and start using them!

Database tools

Although Symfony provides you with the statistics of how quick it retrieves the results from your database, what happens if you see one or two queries that for some reason seem to run slower than expected? There is a useful tool which every developer should know of, that is the explain command.

This shows you how the MySQL query optimizer decides to execute queries. Although it's not entirely accurate, it will give you enough information of where to start looking. To use explain, enter the word explain inside the MySQL client followed by the select statement, which you can copy from the web debug toolbar. For example, if we visit the menu page and click on the database icon in the web debug toolbar, we can see the main query:

```
SELECT milkshakes.ID, milkshakes.NAME, milkshakes.URL_SLUG,
    milkshakes.IMAGE_URL, milkshakes.THUMB_URL,
    milkshakes.CALORIES, milkshakes.VIEWS, milkshakes.CREATED_AT,
    milkshakes.UPDATED_AT FROM `milkshakes` LIMIT 6
```

If we copy this and then enter the query after typing in the `explain` statement as follows:

```
explain SELECT milkshakes.ID, milkshakes.NAME, milkshakes.URL_SLUG,
           milkshakes.IMAGE_URL, milkshakes.THUMB_URL,
           milkshakes.CALORIES, milkshakes.VIEWS,
           milkshakes.CREATED_AT, milkshakes.UPDATED_AT
           FROM `milkshakes` LIMIT 6
```

We end up with a table like the one shown in this screenshot:

```
mysql> explain SELECT milkshakes.ID, milkshakes.NAME, milkshakes.URL_SLUG,
    -> milkshakes.IMAGE_URL, milkshakes.THUMB_URL, milkshakes.CALORIES,
    -> milkshakes.VIEWS, milkshakes.CREATED_AT, milkshakes.UPDATED_AT FROM
    -> `milkshakes` LIMIT 6
    -> ;
+----+-------------+------------+------+---------------+------+---------+------+------+-------+
| id | select_type | table      | type | possible_keys | key  | key_len | ref  | rows | Extra |
+----+-------------+------------+------+---------------+------+---------+------+------+-------+
|  1 | SIMPLE      | milkshakes | ALL  | NULL          | NULL | NULL    | NULL |    9 |       |
+----+-------------+------------+------+---------------+------+---------+------+------+-------+
1 row in set (0.00 sec)
```

 As there are lots of options to look out for, you can find out more information at `http://dev.mysql.com/doc/refman/5.0/en/using-explain.html`.

Deciding on your table types

Another important point to consider before starting is deciding what MySQL table type you are going to use. There is a fair choice, but two of the most popular ones are:

- **MyISAM**: It is mainly for non-transactional tables and provides high-speed storage and retrieval.

- **InnoDB**: InnoDB is ACID compliant. This means that it is transactional. Transactions are safe, but do have more over heads. This is the default table type in Symfony.

Of course, both have pros and cons, so it is worth looking into the table types before starting. Although InnoDB is the default, to change to another table type is a simple matter of inserting the type into the `propel.ini` file, which is located in the `config/` folder.

Accelerators

When a request goes to the web server, the server has to read the script and then execute it. This alone causes a great deal of overhead. When a request is sent through Symfony, a great amount of PHP is interpreted by the server. Symfony, as you have seen, can limit this by caching. However, there are other ways to help combat this by means of a PHP accelerator. An accelerator parses the PHP code, and then compiles the code into bytecode before storing it in the cache. Therefore, it saves time on the server because the PHP scripts are not parsed but only executed. Some good accelerators that you might want to deploy on your production server are:

- eAccelerator—`http://eaccelerator.net/`
- Xcache—`http://xcache.lighttpd.net/`
- Alternative PHP Cache (APC)—`http://uk3.php.net/apc/`
- ionCube PHP Accelerator—`http://www.ioncube.com/`
- Zend Encoder/Guard Platform—`http://www.zend.com/products/guard`

memcached

`memcached` is slightly different from accelerators such as those mentioned in the previous section. This is a memory object caching system. This means that all data and objects are stored in the system memory, which is much faster than caching to the file system. This was created by "Danga", who were at the time suffering performance issues with their web site `Livejournal.com` as it had reached more than 20 million page views a day (see `http://www.danga.com/memcached/`).

Changing the caching framework in our development environment is simply a matter of changing the current settings. Therefore, add the following in the `factories.yml` (`/apps/frontend/config/factories.yml`) file:

```
test:
all:
  routing:
    class: sfPatternRouting
    param:
      generate_shortest_url:          true
      extra_parameters_as_query_string: true
  view_cache:
    class: sfMemcacheCache
      param:
      prefix: frontend
      storeCacheInfo: true
# all:
```

Now delete the cache:

`$/home/timmy/workspace/milkshake>symfony cc`

 Please note that in order for this to work, you must have memcached installed on your local computer and the memcached module enabled in your php.ini.

Essentially, we have just configured the caching framework to sfMemcacheCache rather than using the default sfFileCache. Although we are using the Symfony sfMemcacheCache class, there are other classes available to access the aforementioned accelerators:

- sfAPCCache.class.php
- sfFunctionCache.class.php
- sfSQLiteCache.class.php
- sfEAcceleratorCache.class.php
- sfMemcacheCache.class.php
- sfXCacheCache.class.php
- sfFileCache.class.php
- sfNoCache.class.php

All of these classes extend the sfCache base class, which means that if we want to incorporate another caching method, we can implement our own caching class.

Before we can truly see this working (and I do not mean by the command line), there is a graphical tool that you can download from http://livebookmark. net/journal/2008/05/21/memcachephp-stats-like-apcphp/. After you have downloaded the compressed file, copy the memcache.php file into the web root directory web/. After refreshing the locations page several times, browse to http://milkshake/memcache.php where you will see this:

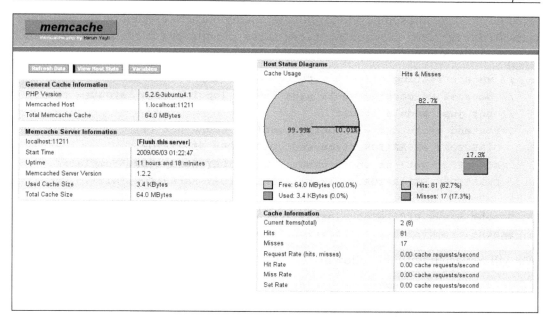

If you clicked on the **Variables** link, then a slab id is followed by the link. In the info column, you would see the following:

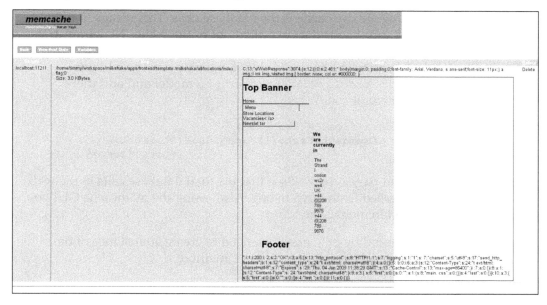

Looking at the screenshot, the locations cache is now being cached in memcache.

Now we need to add some code to allow removing of cache created by the `memcache` class. In the `lib/forms/StoreLocation.class.php` file we edited earlier, we need to remove the following part:

```
// we are setting directory to to <env>/template/milkshake/all,
// because we caching whole page layout (option with_layout = true,
// not just module itself
$frontend_cache_dir = sfConfig::get('sf_cache_dir').
  DIRECTORY_SEPARATOR.'frontend'.DIRECTORY_SEPARATOR.
  sfConfig::get('sf_environment').DIRECTORY_SEPARATOR.'template'.
  DIRECTORY_SEPARATOR.'milkshake'.DIRECTORY_SEPARATOR.'all';

$cache = new sfFileCache(array('cache_dir' => $frontend_cache_dir));
$cache->removePattern('location/index');
```

We will replace it with the following:

```
$cache = new sfMemcacheCache(array('prefix' => 'frontend',
                                   'storeCacheInfo' => true));
$cache->removePattern('/milkshake/all/location/index');
```

Caching database calls

Sometimes the only thing we can cache is the database calls. This means that the database is not queried and the results are pulled out of the cache. To demonstrate this, let's cache the database calls on the menu pages. Because we have the DbFinderPlugin already installed and are using it, we only need to add one adjustment. Open the `lib/models/MilkShakPeer.php` model and add the following highlighted piece of code:

```
$pagerObj = DbFinder::from('Milkshake')->
  useCache(new sfMemcacheCache())->paginate($currentPage,
                                            $totalItems);
```

After revisiting the menu page, you will see that the total database calls in the web debug toolbar has decreased from three to one. Also, using the memcache GUI you can see the results object in memcache too.

To remove the cache created by `DbFinder`, we need to create an instance of the `sfMemcacheCache` class and execute the `clean()` method:

```
$cache = new sfMemcacheCache();
$cache->clean();
```

Summary

Symfony is generally great for web application of any size. However, as a developer, you should always think about scaling your application. Throughout this chapter, we have looked at how we can compress the response and send it back to the user's browser. This alone showed us that the page size was drastically reduced. Moving on to speeding up the processing of our application, we introduced Symfony's caching framework, which again sped up the response time. Finally, we easily configured Symfony to use a memcached server, rather than the default file-based caching. This not only sped up the application, but also showed how we can potentially reduce the database and application processing by serving content from the system memory. Of course, there is nothing stopping you from using `memcached` along with XCache.

Besides looking at how we can configure Symfony to use caching and compression, we looked at several other useful tools to aid in speeding up your web applications.

10
Final Tweaks and Deployment

We have our web site working on our local machine. It is now time to consider deploying the web site to a development, staging, and possibly, a production server. But before we do this, there are a few little tweaks that we should look at.

In this chapter you will learn:

- A better way to transfer your application than using FTP
- Why a standalone application is needed
- How to disable an application to allow you to perform maintenance
- How to customize the default error 404 and error 500 Symfony pages

Editing the default pages

There are a number of default pages that you should skin to match your site; otherwise, they will be Symfony branded. These include the error 404 page, the error 500 page, and the maintenance and security pages.

Apart from the error 500 page and the unavailable page, the rest are all located in Symfony's default module. Therefore, to change these pages, we can follow one of these two options:

- In your Symfony installation, there is a default module. For example, the default module on my installation is located in the `/usr/share/php/data/symfony/modules/default` directory. If you copy this entire folder into your frontend and backend application folders, it will override Symfony's module in the installation. This default module contains all of the default actions and templates for the error 404, login, secure, unavailable, and disabled pages.

- You can amend the application's settings to reflect your specific locations located in the `apps/app_name/config/settings.yml` file. As you can see from the file below, we can uncomment and place references to our own modules instead as follows:

```
all:

  .actions:

# default_module:        default   # Default module and action
to be called when

#     default_action:        index     # A routing rule doesn't
set it
# error_404_module:      default   # To be called when a 404
error is raised

#   error_404_action:      error404  # Or when the requested URL
doesn't match any route
#     login_module:          default   # To be called when a non-
authenticated user
#     login_action:          login     # Tries to access a secure
page
#
#     secure_module:         default   # To be called when a user
doesn't have
#     secure_action:         secure    # The credentials required
for an action
#
#     module_disabled_module: default  # To be called when a user
requests

#     module_disabled_action: disabled # A module disabled in the
module.yml
#
#     unavailable_module:    default   # To be called when a user
requests a page

#     unavailable_action:  unavailable # From an application
disabled via the available setting below
```

I find it easier to copy the default module over to my applications, and amend the templates and action.

The error 500 page and the unavailable page are slightly different. This is because they are called either when there is a major problem, or when your application is down due to clearing cache, for example. To customize these pages, we must create a folder in the application's `config/` folder called `error/`. Inside this folder, we can create two pages: `error.html.php` and `unavailable.php`.

Disabling the application

You never want a user to see that your web site is broken or appears not to be working. This generally happens when you have to make certain kinds of updates to your site, for example, modifying the database. Therefore, through the CLI, you can disable an application as well as an environment by using the Symfony `disable` task. First, we must enable Symfony to check for a lock file. This file is created once we have disabled the applications. In our `settings` file located at `apps/frontend/config/settings.yml`, add the following:

```
dev:
  .settings:
    no_script_name:       on
    logging_enabled:      off
    check_lock:           on
```

Now, we can disable our application using the Symfony task, as follows:

```
>symfony project:disable frontend dev
```

Once you have executed this command, all the URLs are routed to the unavailable action in the Symfony's default module. The following screenshot shows the default unavailable page that is shown if we try to access our `dev` environment:

You can customize the layout of this page in one of these two ways:

- If you have copied the default module over to your application module's folder, you can amend the `unavailableSuccess.php` template to fit in with your style.
- You can edit the application settings in the `apps/frontend/config/settings.yml` file, and point the action and module to a custom module and an action that will handle it.

Consider the following example:

```
all:
  .settings:
    unavailable_module:    mymodule
    unavailable_action:    maintenance
```

From this example, you can see how we could use our own module and action.

The size of your application will determine the amount of time that is required to clear the cache. The more the cache, the longer will it take to clear. Of course, if you start to clear the cache while a user is trying to access the pages, you run the risk of the user seeing a broken web site. Disabling your site will help prevent this. But it is very easy to forget to do this, especially for just clearing the cache.

In the application's `settings` file, there is a `check_lock` option that will add a lock file while the `clear-cache` task is running. This will automatically display the unavailable page while the cache is being deleted. For this to work you must explicitly call the `clear-cache` task and not manually delete the cache using `rm -rf cache/*`. Otherwise, Symfony will not generate the locks and, therefore, this will not work.

Symfony on the server or not?

In Chapter 1, I had mentioned about the different approaches for installing Symfony. To recap, Symfony can be set up in three different ways. You can:

- Download the Sandbox
- Use the SVN externals within your applications
- Install the PEAR package

As our installation of Symfony for this project is done by using the Sandbox, you may have opted for PEAR installation on you local system. Therefore, you could use this approach on the server too. However, if you have web applications written using different versions of Symfony on your production server, it can be a nightmare. Hence, we choose this method because as time goes on, applications can be written using the previous versions of Symfony. Secondly, if you have to deploy your application onto a shared hosting environment, it means the whole project must be packaged up.

Transferring your application to the server

Traditionally, most developers have always used an FTP client to upload their files to the server. The problem with this approach is that it can be very time-consuming, especially if you have several files from different directories. Also, unless you are using a secure FTP sever, the information transferred could potentially be stolen. We will take a look at an alternative method, which is extremely simple to use, and gets the job done faster and more securely.

rsync

rsync is one of the best deployment/backup tools. Basically, it synchronizes one location with another; in our case, our local area with the development area on the remote server. Not only does it provide a simple way to synchronize your files, but it also has plenty of options by which we can synchronize the files. For example, we can choose to transfer the files and folders using compression, or to not transfer any of the hidden versioning folders. Another important feature is that it can use SSH tunneling to enable secure transmission.

If you type `rsync` at the CLI, you will be presented with many options. Here I will only cover the ones that are most commonly used:

```
>rsync

-z: compress file during transfer

-v: Increased verbose

-C: Ignore CVS files/folders

-r: Recursice into directories

-u: Skip files that are newer on the reciever

-d: Transfer dirs without recursion

-t: Preserve times

-n: Dry run
, only show what will be synchronized
-m: Prune empty dirs

-l: copy symlinks as symlinks

-p: preserve permissions

-h: human readable numbers

-g: preserve group
-r: recursive
--progress: Show the progress
--delete: Delete files that don't exist on the sending side
-- exclude
```

We can synchronize our site using some of these switches. Entering the command shown next will synchronize our site. The backslashes allow for multiline commands.

```
>rsync -zlvhvC \
>--delete --progress --force \
>--exclude "/doc/" \
>--exclude "/cache/" \
>--exclude ".*" \
>--exclude "/log/" \
>--exclude "/config/"
>--exclude "web/uploads/"
>.
>username@host.com:/var/www/app-dir
```

 rsync is a unix tool, however, you can find a port for Windows.

Synchronizing does not mean that we must synchronize all of the folders. For example, I have excluded the doc, cache, log, and config folders. After specifying all of the switches and options, you have to specify the base directory and the directory to be synchronized with it. Of course, you can also reverse the locations to synchronize a remote location with a local location for backup purposes.

 Although the folders are excluded, you will need these folders on the server initially.

Symfony and rsync

Having mentioned the benefits of rsync, Symfony too incorporates a task for using rsync to synchronize your project. Configuring Symfony to use rsync requires a few small configuration settings and some settings for excluding certain files.

First, we have to specify all of the connection parameters that rsync requires so that it can connect to the remote server. These settings are located in the config/properties.ini file:

```
[dev]
  host=xxx.xxx.xxx.xxx
  port=22
  user=developers
  dir=/var/www/vhosts/milkshake/httpdocs
```

```
  parameters="-rlzcC --force --delete --no-p --no-t --no-g --no-o --
exclude-from=config/rsync_exclude.txt"

[staging]
  host=xxx.xxx.xxx.xxx
  port=22
  user=root
  dir=/var/www/vhosts/milkshake/httpdocs
  parameters="-rlzcC --force --delete --no-p --no-t --no-g --no-o --
exclude-from=config/rsync_exclude.txt"
```

In the `properties` file, you can have multiple places to synchronize. In this example, I have specified a development and staging environment along with all the connection and parameter details.

We must also add any file and/or folder that should be excluded from synchronizing to the `config/rsync_exclude.txt` file.

Initially, we must synchronize every file and folder apart from the `.svn` folders. Our file will, therefore, resemble the following:

```
.svn
/web/uploads/*
```

Now that all the settings have been entered, you can use the Symfony task to see what will be synchronized (dry run). Type in the following to see what files will be copied over to the `dev` server:

>symfony project:deploy dev

This command will only show you what is going to be synchronized with the `dev` server that we specified. To synchronize your project, add the `--go` switch at the end of the command as shown here:

>symfony project:deploy dev --go

Now that everything is synchronized, we can go ahead and ignore all the files and folders that we do not want to resynchronize. The excluded files are stored in the `config/rsync_exclude.txt` file:

```
.svn

/web/uploads/*
/cache/*
/log/*
/config/databases.yml
/config/*.save
/config/*.ini
```

```
/config/*.txt
/config/*.xml
/config/vhost.sample
/web/googlehostedservice.html
```

> After everything is done, you might need to reset the permission on the `cache` and `web/uploads` folders.
>
> At the time of writing, I found an interesting URL, `http://Symfony-check.org/en/`, that consists of a final checklist.

Finally, make sure that all the settings that we have enabled only in the `dev` environment are now in the production environment too.

> Although rsync is great, you may want something a little more better for deploying you application. One such tool is Capistrano, for more information please see `http://en.wikipedia.org/wiki/Capistrano`.

Summary

This concludes how to deploy and disable your applications. Using rsync is very convenient and fast, as opposed to FTP. Also, although we have used rsync to synchronize to the `dev` server (and perhaps the staging area), it's not a good idea to use this method for a live production area.

Throughout the book, we have taken a journey on how Symfony aids us in rapid application development. Looking at the main features again, we can see that:

- The use of Symfony CLI tasks helps generate modules, projects, and forms
- We can tap into a vast amount of plugins and also refactor our own modules to create our own plugins
- Configuration files make Symfony extremely flexible
- The ORM layer makes communicating with the database easy
- Integration with third-party libraries can be seamless
- Creating a multilingual site is very simple

With all of these features, Symfony does, in fact, provide a tightly-coded rapid-application framework.

Index

translation dictionary file 160
doSelect() function 155
dynamic pages
    caching 184

E

entity tag. *See* **Etag**
ETag 187
executeBatch() function 114
executeBatchDelete() function 114
executeDelete() function 114
executeEdit() function 114
executeIndex() function 114
executeNew() function 114
executeUpdate() function 114
eZ Component
    about 167
    configuring, with Symfony 168, 169
    downloading 168
    graph component, using 167
    using 169-171

F

filters
    generating 27, 28
Firefox developer tools, aid tools
    Firebug 189
    Firephp 189
    Web developer tools 189
    Yslow 189
fixtures file 44
folder structure skeleton, creating
    Doctorine file structure, generating 16
    frontend application folder structure,
        generating 18
    project, viewing 20
    project/apps, top level folders 19
    project file structure, generating 16
    project folder, creating 16
    project folder, top-level folders 18
    Symfony tasks 16
foreign key
    application settings, accessing 122, 123
    handling, admin generator used 119-121
    partials used, in generated views 123

form
    base form class 78
    base form class, features 79
    binding, to database table 77
    form validators, adding 84
    form widgets, modifying 83
    generating 27, 28
    global rendering, changing 87, 88
    naming convention 85
    rendering 80, 81
    rendering, customizing 89
    security 91, 92
    style, setting 85
    submitting 85, 86
    unneeded fields, removing 83
    validators, customizing 82
    widgets, customizing 82
form rendering customization
    email section, customizing 89-91
form style
    setting 85
form validators
    adding 84
    SfValidatorEmail 84
    SfValidatorPropelChoice 84
    SfValidatorPropelUnique 84
    sfValidatorString 84
form widgets
    customizing 82, 83
frontend_dev.php controller
    using 39

G

generated models
    about 43, 44
    custom class 44
    database, populating 44, 45
    non-peer class 43
    peer class 43
generators 11
getCulture() method 155
getPreferredCulture() method 156
getVacancies() method
    creating 155

Thank you for buying
Symfony 1.3
Web Application Development

Packt Open Source Project Royalties

When we sell a book written on an Open Source project, we pay a royalty directly to that project. Therefore by purchasing Symfony 1.3 Web Application Development, Packt will have given some of the money received to the Symfony project.

In the long term, we see ourselves and you—customers and readers of our books—as part of the Open Source ecosystem, providing sustainable revenue for the projects we publish on. Our aim at Packt is to establish publishing royalties as an essential part of the service and support a business model that sustains Open Source.

If you're working with an Open Source project that you would like us to publish on, and subsequently pay royalties to, please get in touch with us.

Writing for Packt

We welcome all inquiries from people who are interested in authoring. Book proposals should be sent to author@packtpub.com. If your book idea is still at an early stage and you would like to discuss it first before writing a formal book proposal, contact us; one of our commissioning editors will get in touch with you.

We're not just looking for published authors; if you have strong technical skills but no writing experience, our experienced editors can help you develop a writing career, or simply get some additional reward for your expertise.

About Packt Publishing

Packt, pronounced 'packed', published its first book "Mastering phpMyAdmin for Effective MySQL Management" in April 2004 and subsequently continued to specialize in publishing highly focused books on specific technologies and solutions.

Our books and publications share the experiences of your fellow IT professionals in adapting and customizing today's systems, applications, and frameworks. Our solution-based books give you the knowledge and power to customize the software and technologies you're using to get the job done. Packt books are more specific and less general than the IT books you have seen in the past. Our unique business model allows us to bring you more focused information, giving you more of what you need to know, and less of what you don't.

Packt is a modern, yet unique publishing company, which focuses on producing quality, cutting-edge books for communities of developers, administrators, and newbies alike. For more information, please visit our website: www.PacktPub.com.

Zend Framework 1.8 Web Application Development

ISBN: 978-1-847194-22-0   Paperback: 350 pages

Create powerful web applications by leveraging the power of this Model-View-Controller-based framework

1. Learn by doing – create a "real-life" storefront application

2. Covers access control, performance optimization, and testing

3. Best practices, as well as debugging and designing discussion

CakePHP Application Development

ISBN: 978-1-847193-89-6   Paperback: 332 pages

Step-by-step introduction to rapid web development using the open-source MVC CakePHP framework

1. Develop cutting-edge Web 2.0 applications, and write PHP code in a faster, more productive way

2. Walk through the creation of a complete CakePHP Web application

3. Customize the look and feel of applications using CakePHP layouts and views

4. Make interactive applications using CakePHP, JavaScript, and AJAX helpers

Please check **www.PacktPub.com** for information on our titles

CodeIgniter for Rapid PHP Application Development

ISBN: 978-1-847191-74-8   Paperback: 260 pages

Improve your PHP coding productivity with the free compact open-source MVC CodeIgniter framework!

1. Clear, structured tutorial on working with CodeIgniter

2. Careful explanation of the basic concepts of CodeIgniter and its MVC architecture

3. Using CodeIgniter with databases, HTML forms, files, images, sessions, and email

4. Building a dynamic website quickly and easily using CodeIgniter's prepared code

PHP 5 CMS Framework Development

ISBN: 978-1-847193-57-5   Paperback: 348 pages

Expert insight and practical guidance to creating an efficient, flexible, and robust framework for a PHP 5-based content management system

1. Learn how to design, build, and implement a complete CMS framework for your custom requirements

2. Implement a solid architecture with object orientation, MVC

3. Build an infrastructure for custom menus, modules, components, sessions, user tracking, and more

4. Written by a seasoned developer of CMS applications

Please check **www.PacktPub.com** for information on our titles